AF271314

Summer Camp Rules!

Thirty Years of Practical Wisdom from Bob Ditter

Bob Ditter

ISBN: 978-1-60679-165-3
Library of Congress Control Number: 2011921900
Cover design: Roger W. Rybkowski
Layout design: Roger W. Rybkowski
Cover photos: Meri Bond Photography

Healthy Learning
P.O. Box 1828
Monterey, CA 93942
www.healthylearning.com

Contents

Key point #1:   Be aware that nonverbal communication counts.

Key point #2:   Make eye contact.

Key point #3:   Smile!

Key point #4:   Be on the same physical level.

Key point #5:   Know the "three safe places" to touch a child—
                the advantages of light physical touch.

Key point #6:   Develop a "look" of your own.

Key point #7:   Develop a second "look"—praise.

Key point #8:   A word about praising teens

Key point #9:   You have two relationships with teenagers.

Key point #10: Learn about each camper.

Key point #11: Encourage new friendships.

Key point #12: Move toward your campers.

Key point #13: Drop the rope—a master skill.

Key point #14: State what you expect in positive terms
                (the brain can't hold a negative).

Key point #15: Thank younger kids first for doing what you ask them to do.

Dedication

This book is dedicated to Ray and Linda Diamond, whose trust, wisdom, warmth, and friendship have nurtured and inspired me from the very first day we met.

Acknowledgments

I thank my editor, Theresa Litz, for her sharp and timely help; Jim Peterson at Healthy Learning, who has always been encouraging and supportive of my work; Harriet Lowe at *Camping Magazine,* whose friendship, support, and professionalism are invaluable to me; and all the camp professionals who have shared their stories and passion for camp with me over the years. I especially thank Jay and Mindy Jacobs for trusting me as a member of their family of camps; Dan and Jane Kagan, who have become good friends; all the good folks in Mentone, Alabama, who every year host a "Bob Ditter Day;" Bob and Marcy Brower, who have been teaching me for over 25 years; the Cheley clan in Estes Park for being such strong supporters; my tireless cheerleader, June Gray; and Lillian Ussher, who still inspires me from the great beyond. There are so many wonderful camp friends to name that once I start I am afraid I will leave someone out. Your combined commitment to the young people of this country has always inspired me.

I also thank my sister, Jennifer Williams, for her unconditional love and encouragement when I needed it most.

Above all, I thank Alphonse for his unending love, loyalty, and friendship, without which I would still be typing in the dark.

Preface

"Have You Been What...?"

"I came to get Ditter-ized!"

To be honest, I'm not sure when I first heard someone use that line. I do know it was just before the beginning of one of the numerous sessions I have done at various local, regional, and national camp conferences since 1981. One of the many camp professionals I have been fortunate to get to know over the years came up to the front of the room and announced that he had come for what he called "being Ditter-ized."

Starting somewhere back in the early 1990s, counselors at some of the camps I visited during the summer would announce at the end of a training session, "Well, now I've been Ditter-ized!" The term has stuck to a point where even today, perhaps 20 years after I first heard it, the phrase, "Have you been Ditter-ized?" is something many counselors at camps all across the United States recognize.

So just what does it mean to "get Ditter-ized?" The original meaning of the phrase came from trainings I was conducting in the late 1980s about child safety. In them, I outlined what constituted appropriate contact between campers and staff. It was at the end of a decade when a lot of high profile child abuse cases had been in the news and camp professionals were scrambling to put standards of conduct in place that would assure parents that their children would be safe from sexual or physical abuse at camp. Among the areas I spoke about were "the three safe places" to touch a child you didn't know; not touching a child anywhere on their body that would normally be covered by a bathing suit; not being alone with a camper and out of the sight of other adults; and a host of other things that were intended to ensure that camp remain a safe place for kids. Learning and practicing these guidelines became known as being "Ditter-ized."

Since the 1980s, the term "to be Ditter-ized" has been more broadly associated with a firm but empathic way of working with children. It has to do with listening to children, truly being present and developing a caring relationship with them that serves as the main vehicle for influencing their behavior. Indeed, to be "Ditter-ized" implies an understanding that in our work with children, whether at camp or in school or other setting, we do not control children's behavior so much as we influence their behavior.

To be "Ditter-ized" means comprehending that as human beings we always inhabit two worlds: that of feelings, which people often refer to as our "heart," and what psychologists call our irrational side; and our mind, or our rational side. Being "Ditter-ized" means striking a balance between validating, or acknowledging a child's feelings, and holding them to as high a level of behavior as possible, given their particular circumstances and stage of development.

One of the simple examples I give of this balance is when a child accidently bumps into or hurts another child. Most children who are hurt aren't interested in whether it was an accident or not; they just feel hurt and angry, and they often just want revenge. Acknowledging the legitimacy of that feeling or impulse while still setting a limit ("it's okay to have angry feelings, it's not okay to hit your friends!") is central to this approach. I suppose being "Ditter-ized" most closely follows what some people call the "authoritative" style of parenting, one of the three styles of parenting described by Diana Baumrind. (Baumrind, D., 1971. "Current patterns of parental authority." *Developmental Psychology,* 4, pp. 1-103). She suggests that three main parenting styles exist: authoritarian or "strict" (telling children exactly what to do); permissive (allowing children to do whatever they wish); or authoritative (providing rules and guidance without being overbearing). I think of parenting as a kind of benevolent dictatorship in that parents always have the final say. As I have rhetorically asked in the past, "whoever said children always know what's in their best interest?" Parents who are authoritative are nurturing in the sense that they are understanding of and responsive to their children's emotional needs without being held hostage by them.

Authoritative parents set limits and demand maturity, but when responding to a child's misbehavior, the parent will explain what was inappropriate about the behavior and will issue a consequence to the child. Consequences are measured and consistent, rather than harsh or arbitrary, and are designed to help the child see that all behavior is the result of making a "choice." Authoritative parents teach children that all choices have consequences. Authoritative parents set clear standards for their children, monitor limits that they set, and encourage their children to develop autonomy. They also expect children to exhibit mature, independent, and age-appropriate behavior. They are attentive to their children's needs and concerns, and will typically forgive and teach, instead of punishing a child if he or she misbehaves. Authoritative parenting results in children who have higher self-esteem and a greater degree of independence because of the mix of nurturing, empathy, and appropriate limit setting. It is the parenting style that most closely reflects what it means to "be Ditter-ized."

In the 30 years that I have been working with camp professionals, I have developed numerous techniques for working with children in the camp setting. Those techniques and strategies, many of which are presented in this book, are part of what it means to "be Ditter-ized." Happy reading.

1

A Word to Camp Professionals: The Demands of Being a Camp Professional in a Brave New World

Jupiterimages

When I first started visiting a group of camps on Lookout Mountain in Mentone, Alabama, back in 1987, a camp director and now good friend, Rob Hammond, explained to me how staff training had been conducted at Camp Laney for Boys in the late 1950s and early '60s.

"All the counselors would come up to camp the week before it opened for what was called work week, which was really five days of getting the camp grounds ready for the summer," he explained. "We would put the docks in down at the river, get the canoes and other equipment out of winter storage, and get the basketball and tennis nets up. Other guys would cut the fields and lime the foul lines for baseball and football, while still others would sweep out the gym or bring the horses in and get the stables ready. We'd inventory what was needed and go into town for whatever gear we needed for the new season. It was a busy, physical week, peppered with spirited games of 'bombardy' (bombardment) and basketball up in the gym, and featuring meals fit for guys working hard in the heat. On Sunday, the day the campers were due to arrive, we would have what was called morning watch, our camp version of a spiritual service, then head into the lodge for a big breakfast. Later, we would assemble on the porch of the lodge and listen to Coach Laney talk to us about the campers. He would say, 'Well, boys, the campers are soon to arrive. Let's all have a great summer and remember—be friendly, firm, and fair!' That was the essence of staff training 50 years ago."

When I was a camp counselor in the 1970s, staff training was still very much like Camp Laney 20 years earlier. We basically put the camp physically together and had a few meetings on the schedule for the day and how the dining hall worked, but nothing in depth about interacting and working with kids. When I entered the camp scene as a consultant and trainer in the early 1980s, the widespread practice of directors was to hold staff training sessions, usually in the way of informal meetings in the lodge or dining hall, where counselors would amp up on caffeine to keep from nodding off during the interminable lectures on various aspects of camp culture. It was all very top-down learning, and if we were lucky, the staff retained about 10 percent of what they heard that week.

Beginning in the mid-1980s, a change began to take place, where staff orientation became more experiential. At the urging of a group of trainers—and by then consultants like me—directors began to use icebreakers and team-building exercises to liven up staff training. It was an exciting development. Groups went up the "pamper pole" or over "the wall," while teams of counselors figured out how to get everyone across the "valley of poison peanut butter," carrying a pail of "nitroglycerin" (water) on a rope swing down at the ropes course most every camp had scrambled to build in the 1980s and '90s. Games were added that were designed to promote group cohesion among the staff, while also serving as practice runs for teaching the campers new activities. While the activities were fun, whether they actually improved the skill level of staff is debatable. But in a more dynamic environment where counselors were encouraged to participate in orientation, they were definitely motivated to stay awake—and listen. The camp training session that ended with the mantra, "be friendly, firm and fair," was officially a thing of the past.

In the meantime, the behavior that camp professionals were witnessing in children in the early 1990s seemed to be getting more and more challenging. One phenomenon affecting that behavior is television. In her article, "The Effects of Technological Overload on Children: An Art Therapist's Perspective," P. Gussie Klorer states that one-year-olds in the United States are already watching an average of 2.2 hours of television a day. By the time they are three years old, that average rises to 3.6 hours a day. By the time kids are 10 years old, they are watching an average of four hours of television a day. And while parents often ban such shows as *South Park, Gossip Girls, Jersey Shore,* and *Family Guy,* and adult shows where the insults fly and sex and rude behavior are as common as sunscreen in July, they feel resigned to the fact that their kids will probably end up watching those same shows on their friends' TiVo® or some other child's i-Phone®.

Consider the show *South Park.* Created for mature audiences and known for its crude, satirical, and dark humor, *South Park* is a show about kids, but definitely not *for* kids. Thanks to the invention of TiVo, "smart phones," and an increasingly permissive parenting style, however, many children see it anyway. The phrase, "you're not the boss of me," first uttered by one of the four main animated child characters when the show debuted in 1997, was mimicked by hundreds of children in schools and camps all over the country. It is only one example of the kind of rude, provocative camper behavior counselors were being confronted with.

Nowadays, children show up at camp with what seems like an alphabet soup of possible behavioral or emotional maladies, all of which have their attendant abbreviations and medications. The array of childhood disorders is dizzying, with clinical labels like Asperger's Syndrome, ADHD, OCD, Bipolar disorder, or Tourettes Syndrome. More and more camper health forms come with the suspicious sounding parental description, "has an inquisitive, independent mind." (Code for, "Good luck! Let's see if you have more success with him than we as parents do!"). The "meds call" after breakfast quickly became the new "first activity period" at a lot of camps. As a result, what counselors now need and what parents expect is a skill level working with their children that is far greater than even 10 years ago. In an age when parents are terrified about the ill will in the world—abductions, child abuse, violence, and the now pervasive and all-purpose evil of "bullying," it's a miracle that parents still allow their children to go to camp. Once there, counselors need to able to cope with and respond to challenging camper behavior in a way that is reassuring to parents, while retaining the fun that is camp. What has emerged is a new emphasis on creating an environment at camp that is physically and emotionally safe, something I named "the envelope of safety." Icebreakers and teambuilding exercises are simply not enough. Indeed, Coach Laney would hardly recognize the world campers and their families inhabit today.

Teambuilding exercises and other cooperative games still play a significant role in staff orientation, but camp professionals have come to realize that their counselors need substantial skills in order to communicate with and manage camper behavior more effectively. This book is one response to that need. Divided into specific sections according to the various ways counselors interact with campers (one-on-one, in groups, and during activities), it is a sampling of tried-and-true skill sets. First, basic ideas and methods of communicating effectively with children are covered, which are expanded and developed into more advanced techniques as the book progresses. Because working with young people requires as much intuition as skill, the first few chapters are devoted to a kind of practical philosophy that will help lead to greater success with children.

Most camp professionals I have met over the past 30 years are people committed to creating meaningful communities for children and young adults, because they are dedicated to helping young people be healthy, self-reliant, thriving, conscientious members of society. Indeed, given all the risks that an individual assumes in taking on the care and welfare of other people's children, I am amazed that there are still folks crazy enough to run summer camps! So, as I say to counselors, if you are going to go into the white water of life with people, as you will surely do when you work with children today, be sure to take the right equipment. The tools, techniques, and approaches in this book are a good start.

Reference

"The Effects of Technological Overload on Children: An Art Therapist's Perspective," P. Gussie Klorer, *Journal of the American Art Therapy Association,* 2009, 26 (2), pp. 80-82.

2

A Word to Staff: It's Not About You. It's All About You!

Jupiterimages

I am standing in the middle of the woodshop of a boys' sailing camp on Cape Cod, examining a hunk of wood that is on its way to becoming a fully functional model sailboat. Suddenly, I hear the ruckus outside. I hand the hull over to the boy who owns it and quickly step onto the shop porch just in time to see Mark, one of my 10-year-old campers, with his back to me threatening to chuck a rock at some kid only a few feet away. "Mark!" I shout at the top of my lungs. Mark, startled by my outburst, whips around and throws the rock *at me.* I somehow manage to duck at the last second, and it whizzes past my right ear, missing me by only inches. Trust me when I say dodging rocks wasn't a skill they asked me about when I interviewed for this job.

The fun started early with my 10-year-old challenger for the summer of 1974. "Mark" (not his real name) arrived at camp with cherry bombs and firecrackers in his trunk. He said they were to "help celebrate the Fourth of July!" From demonstrating the various motions of human reproduction with his pillow to planning disappearances out of the cabin during rest hour, Mark at once appalled, terrified, and delighted his cabin mates. Michael Thompson and Catherine O'Neil Grace in their popular book, *Best Friends, Worst Enemies,* might well describe him as a "controversial child"; that is, he is a kid who definitely gets the attention of his peers but in ways not necessarily popular with them or the adults around them.

I spent the summer taking Mark aside for little chats and time-outs. On days when his behavior was especially "creative," the two of us would row a pram out to the center of the salt water bay where the boys practiced their sailing skills so Mark could give me his undivided attention. There I would tell him *one more time* how he could save himself from being sent home. Aside from the rock-throwing incident, he wasn't so much a danger as he was a test of my patience and imagination. I will tell you, though, that nowhere in staff training was there a *hint* about how I should handle this young man. Even if the camp had known about Mark's behavior ahead of time, they probably wouldn't have divulged any knowledge of it to me for fear that I might bolt before the summer ever started. Even if we had talked about behavior management or communication skills during orientation, the work with Mark would have tested my mettle. Yet, it proved to be the beginning of my life's work as a trainer and camp consultant, developing techniques to help generations of camp professionals be better at what they do.

In the years since my camp counselor days, I have written many articles and given many training sessions on the essential skills camp professionals need to develop in order to work effectively with campers. Some of them, like "drop the rope" and "state your expectations and detach," would probably have helped me with Mark many years ago. Indeed, the seeds of some of those ideas were probably planted over 45 years ago when Mark was demonstrating ever new and imaginative ways of misbehaving. Many of those ideas are included in this book. Learning these concepts is what counselors and directors mean when they say they have been "Ditter-ized!"

Yet, skills alone do not make for an effective camp counselor. There are qualities—abilities and competencies—that you either bring to camp or develop quickly if you are going to be successful (or, in the case of campers like Mark, if you just want to survive).

So, before you start looking at this book of skills, I want to share with you some of the lessons I have learned over the years that contribute to success at camp as a counselor. They are the core principles that have stood the test of time and will contribute to your success as a camp counselor or professional. A heads-up: I will be "talking out of both sides of my mouth!"

Put the Needs of Others Ahead of Your Own. Be Selfish.

When I think of all the terrific camp counselors I have known over the years, it seems they all had one quality in common: their ability to put the needs of others ahead of their own. Being able to step out of your own world and forgo your own comfort and defer your own needs or fun is not something all counselors are willing to do. My hunch about this point was verified by a unique project I had the privilege of participating in several years ago.

Early in the 1990s, a camp director I had developed a close friendship with came to me and said, "Bob, it seems to me that if we are going to deliver a consistently high level of quality care to campers—a way of making kids feel as safe and as well cared for as they might feel at home, then we need a better way to pick truly great counselors. Can you find me a company that knows how to do that?" About a year and several untold thousands of dollars later, we had the answer. I had found a company in Boston that specialized in the art and science of selection. This group had a special ability to develop specific, well-formed critical questions to help identify the *best candidates* in a particular field. In our case, we were looking for the best camp counselors. The way these folks achieved this objective was to hold separate focus groups with the campers, parents, and staff members of this particular camp to discover exactly what were the competencies of the highest performing counselors at camp—the qualities of the best staff.

The project was repeated about three years later, when a group of 22 private independent camps retained the same company. The company then held similar focus groups with campers, parents, and high-performing staff *all over the United States.* The results of this second round of investigation validated the results of the first project. To make a long story short, from the reams of information we collected and analyzed, we determined that *one critical core competency of the best camp counselors is their ability to put the needs of others ahead of their own.* Who gets that last piece of dessert at lunch, you or a camper? Who gets your attention during an activity period, your friend the co-counselor or the campers? When you have a camper who needs a little extra care because she is homesick or having an adjustment problem in her group, do you spend that extra time with the child, even though it may mean you get out of camp for your night off a little later than you normally would? Not everyone is observant or perceptive enough to notice that a child may even be in need, let alone willing to spend the extra time or make the extra effort to attend to those needs. Those counselors who are not only observant and have patience but who *give of themselves* are the ones who set themselves apart at camp. Indeed, most counselors can name the highest performing members of the staff at their camp. It seems everyone in camp knows who those counselors are, not because they broadcast their contributions or brag about their work or good deeds, but because they quietly go about their business in a way that makes everyone notice the difference they make.

The capacity to put the needs of others ahead of your own has as a part of it the natural tendency to be *generous*—that is, to be liberal in sharing your time, energy, enthusiasm, and recognition with others. It also requires you to be *patient*—to understand that children are a work in progress and that staying calm actually *increases* your influence with them. Counselors who give of themselves are not at camp to enhance their own status, feed their own egos, or glorify themselves. They know camp is not about them but about the campers, the community, and protecting the reputation of camp, so that it can continue to be a "safe haven" for campers year after year. (For more on this last point, see Chapter 4).

That said, I learned a long time ago when I was in training as a child and family therapist that I couldn't help anyone if I didn't take good care of myself. Camp is taxing. Campers, in their noisy, messy, always curious, imperfect, impulsive natural state, exert a kind of "regressive pull" on us. That is, their behavior can rub off on us, and if we are not careful, we are at risk of mimicking their noisy, messy, impulsive behavior. Resisting or combating that regression takes a lot of emotional energy. Being in the company of children can be draining. If you don't balance taking care of them with renewing and refreshing yourself, you actually might regress and *start to look and act just like the campers do* in their worst moments. In other words, if you are not well rested and don't take some "down time" away from the kids, you yourself are taking the risk of becoming irritable and impulsive. Taking care of others definitely requires that you take good care of yourself.

One prime example of taking care of yourself is getting enough sleep. Research tells us that we are getting on average about one full hour less sleep a night today than just 20 years ago (Bronson and Merriman, 2009). Lack of sleep over the course of a summer can lead to poor judgment and loss of patience. Be good to yourself. Get some solid rest. and you will be more patient and effective with your campers.

Accept Constructive Feedback. Be Your Own Best Critic.

One of the most difficult, yet useful, abilities for anyone working with children to develop is the capacity to hear and accept constructive feedback. I don't know of anyone who is truly great at what they do who hasn't benefitted from the experience, advice, and knowledge of people who have gone before them. The challenge is that your pride may get in your way of acknowledging that someone else may have something to teach you. Working with children has so many different facets and challenges that there is always more we can all learn about program ideas, behavior management ideas, or just fun ways to pass the time. The greater your "bag of tricks," the more likely you are to stay fresh and continue to be a great counselor or director.

In other words, strong, successful counselors who are committed to excellence become personally engaged in their work. The drawback is that they may get *too* personally engaged in their work. Taking pride in your work cuts both ways. On one hand, taking pride in your work makes you give it your all. It propels you to do a good job. That same pride may also be what prevents you from looking at how you can continue to get better. When someone gives you a pointer, makes a suggestion, or shows you a better way to do something, you have a choice: either you can feel slighted, get defensive, and see their comment as a statement of what you don't know (like a deficit in yourself); or you can see it as an opportunity to add to your repertoire and see if the advice might help you. Getting defensive is a common enough phenomenon, especially at camp, where the efforts of so many good counselors often go unrecognized and unappreciated. The tendency to be defensive may be greater if you are a new or less-experienced camp counselor or if you have a personal history where you were made to feel unappreciated or unseen. Just remember, the people who are the best in their field are those individuals who've been able to accept pointers and learn from all the great folks who've gone before them. Being a camp counselor is no different.

Most of us know when we've done a good job and when we haven't. Be honest with yourself. When you cut corners or don't put in your best effort, it is not only the children (and the camp) you are cheating, but also yourself. Being the best you can be means living up to your "best self," as well as your best teachers, your best mentors, your best friends—all of the people on whose shoulders you stand and whom you carry inside of you who have encouraged, supported, and believed in you. We all have good days and bad days. Those counselors who have a strong, but fair, "self-critic" and who can accept the helpful advice of others are those who learn from their bad days in a way that helps them have an increasing number of good ones!

It's Not About You. It's All about You!

When a camper is rude or defiant or challenges your authority, it would be natural to take it personally or act defensively. After all, you've been encouraged to develop a caring relationship with your campers and work closely with them at camp. Having a camper get under your skin is a hazard of working on such a personal level. Yet, we all know that children bring with them what I call "the other duffel bag"—all the unfinished tasks of growing up, which includes some of the following:

- Learning how to wait
- Recognizing the needs of others
- Respecting authority
- Delaying gratification
- Working together
- Accepting help
- Tolerating conflict
- Recovering from a setback

Take a good look at the aforementioned list. There is a lot for kids to learn, and the process goes on for many years. Campers will undoubtedly practice their life lessons on you, other counselors, and on their friends. The less secure you are about yourself and where you stand with your own peers, the more vulnerable you will be to the camper challenges that will undoubtedly come your way. The less secure you are, the more you will tend to go along with some inappropriate camper behavior, like gossiping or playing favorites, or the more likely you will be to view inappropriate camper behavior as personal affront.

As the counselor, you are the adult. You are the individual who maintains a sense of safety and fairness in your cabin, tent, or group. Even when campers test your limits, subconsciously, they are counting on you to be the more mature and responsible person. When they are being childish and immature, they need you to be the grownup. If you react to provocative camper behavior the way that a child would, there is little hope that they can learn civil, more mature conduct, which is why I say camp is not *about you.* Rather, it is about the development of character, or the "growing up," of your campers who may use you as a kind of surrogate parent—a mentor and a role model— to work out some of their own issues on their way to becoming more mature.

What this means is that the success of camp is *all* about you. It is about your personal commitment to give of yourself, to bring the program to life, to inspire and encourage your campers; to temper their impulses by tempering yours, and to teach them respect, patience, and empathy by *being* respectful, patient, and empathic. Such qualities—respect, patience, fairness, and empathy—are learned only through experience, by being in the company of people who are respectful, patient, fair, and empathic. Studies tell us over and over again that the single greatest factor assuring that young people grow up to be self-respecting, productive human beings who re able to love and care for others is the presence of a significant, caring adult in their lives.

When Mark arrived at camp over 35 years ago, he didn't have much patience, empathy, or respect for others. Working with him that summer helped me develop those same qualities not only in him, but also in myself.

References

Thompson, M.; O'Neill Grace, C.; and Cohen, L.J. (2001). *Best Friends, Worst Enemies—Understanding the Social Lives of Children.* Ballantine Books, New York.

Bronson, P. and Merryman A. (2009). *NurtureShock: New Thinking about Children,* Twelve, Hachette Book Group, New York, Boston.

3

How Hard Can this Possibly Be?
The Art and Craft
of Being a Camp Counselor

Jupiterimages

From time to time while I am at a camp doing staff training, I run across a counselor who questions the need to have an outside professional like me come to their camp to talk about working with kids for the summer. "Just how hard could this possibly be?" one young man once asked me. "I mean, you get together with a bunch of kids and do fun stuff at a place with great facilities, while other people make your meals and take care of the place. Aren't we making too much of this?"

If you are an experienced camp counselor or camp professional, you probably have a wry smile on your face reading that last comment. To be sure, being a camp counselor and hanging out with kids at camp can be a lot of fun. If it weren't, people wouldn't do it year after year to the tune of almost a million counselors and 10 million campers or more every summer. On the other hand, being a camp counselor may be one of the more difficult jobs in the world. Let me explain.

First of all, there are as many ways to be a camp counselor as there are people doing it. There are no lessons you can take—no college practicum or Red Cross course—that will teach you how to be a good counselor. Being a camp counselor is truly *on-the-job training.*

Second, you and your colleagues give up a lot of personal freedom to do this job. Most of you will come from a place just before camp where you had the freedom to decide things, like how late you stayed out at night and how you organized your time. You most likely had a lot of *choices* about whether you showed up for breakfast, what you ate at each meal, whom you sat with, or what time you ate, and on and on. Kiss that entire set of freedoms goodbye. Being in a camp community means giving up a lot of *personal choices.* It means that you have agreed to abide by decisions other people will make about your time and your activities, like what time you get up in the morning, when you eat, what you eat, who sits next to you, what your schedule is, whether you can go out at night, whether and when you get time off, and even who you get to take days off with. If you are a counselor who has come from a college or university setting or your own apartment, this change can be a difficult adjustment to make.

Then, consider the working and living conditions at camp. At day camp, you start *as soon as the kids get on the bus.* Forget that camp hasn't officially begun. Once campers congregate, they start interacting, and that's when camp officially begins. Once you are at camp—day camp or resident camp—even if you have a period off, when a kid is in need, when they have fallen and hurt themselves, like it or not, you are "on!" You can't tell an injured child, "Hey, I'll be right there as soon as my period off is over!" If it is 2 o'clock in the morning and a camper is having a nightmare, you're up—and *on!*

Then, there is the issue of privacy. Camp is a rumor mill. At camp, people work in such close quarters and share so much that if you have something private about yourself, just wait five minutes. By then, the entire community will know your business (or, more likely, some distorted, rumored version of it). Being in a community is especially difficult for Americans, since we are used to having a lot of personal freedom. Having to compromise or give up some of your individual freedom is what it takes to be part of any community, not just camp. At camp, there is always tension between having a mind of your own and being part of a community, where the greater good of the group must take priority.

Finally, there is the work with the campers themselves. As I mentioned in Chapter 2, children in their natural state are noisy, nosey, messy, impulsive, imperfect, and dependent. No wonder your non-camp friends don't recognize you when you return home. Look who you've been hanging out with all summer! The *regressive pull* I described in Chapter 2 can be subtle and exhausting. What happens is that, as human beings, we tend to *mirror* or mimic the behavior of those around us after a while. Being a camp counselor, where you are constantly with campers whose behavior is hardly mature, you may have a tendency to regress. Before you know it, you are acting more like a child than an adult, *and you may not even notice it.* It takes a lot of emotional energy to stay in a mature, centered, thoughtful state of mind, when the pull to regress is all around you.

Children also have a tendency to accuse one another of the very things *they* do wrong. If something they own is missing, they accuse the kid next to them of taking it—only to find it later under a pile of clothes under their bunk. (Even when they find it and all evidence points to the fact that *they* misplaced the item, they may still insist *they* didn't put it there!) Kids can be self-centered and often have trouble waiting their turn, asking for or accepting help, controlling their feelings, and listening to others. When something goes wrong, they are quite skilled at pointing out what others may have done to contribute to the problem. On the other hand, they often have a harder time seeing what role they may have played in it. Then, when you least expect it and are tempted to commit a major felony against them, children can suddenly be the most caring, appreciative, affectionate, funny people in the world, which may be why so many young adults continue to work as counselors year after year, in spite of the sacrifices.

Children also have their own way of looking at the world. I remember being at a YMCA camp in Texas one year, where the dining hall worked like this: every camper went through the cafeteria line to get their food, and then came to two long tables, where there were condiments, salad, and "extras" they could take. On the first table, this particular day, was a huge bowl of beautiful big red apples. Above the apples was a sign that read, "Help yourself but, please, take only ONE! And remember, God is watching!" At the end of the second table was a large plate of freshly baked cookies. Above the cookies, there was also a sign that read, "Please help yourself." The other lines had been crossed out by some teenage comedian, and in place of what had been written, he wrote, "And remember, God is watching the apples!"

Youngsters are a work in progress—which adds up to a lot of work for you, every summer there are different kids. One summer, you might have someone with Tourette's syndrome, or a kid with a hair-trigger temper, or a camper who just doesn't fit into his or her cabin or group. On the other hand, perhaps you'll have a group of kids who just can't share or who fight about the littlest things—or who are all homesick. The truth is, no matter how much information parents put on their "camper behavior forms," you just don't know what your campers will really be like until they get off the bus or come through the front gate. Some camps do a pretty good job of sitting down with counselors beforehand to assess each camper in the group or cabin to give them a "heads-up" about the personalities, habits, or hobbies of the campers. Then again, some parents just don't share the truth about their children. Like the camper who has an extreme bedwetting problem at home that parents think will miraculously disappear when the child comes came to camp. Or the child on stimulant medication for Attention Deficit Hyperactive Disorder (ADHD) whom the parents unilaterally decide to take her off her meds for the summer, even though they will tell you she can't sit still in school for two seconds without it. The truth is that no one knows how each child is going to be at camp in the particular group they have been placed in until the camper actually arrives.

So, while it would be nice to think that you can simply "wing it" as a counselor, the truth is that working effectively with children is no different from most other professional endeavors: It takes skill, practice and patience. Being a camp counselor is a craft. It is a set of skills and talents that, when you practice, you can actually become better at. It takes no skill, insight, self-restraint, or ability simply to "gut react" to kids. Anyone can do that. And when we do, there is no gain, no improvement, no advancement, no better outcome, or no growth to be had. To be thoughtful and respond in a way that makes a difference with a child—where the camper actually learns something that enhances the child's ability to accept help or see someone else's point of view or wait patiently or overcome a fear—takes patience, practice, and skill. And did I mention patience?

That is what this book is all about. It is organized by chapter, according to the different ways you will be interacting with your campers: one-on-one, in their group, and during activities. The skills and tips are organized from very basic to more complex or advanced. That said, the following points are a few things you should keep in mind that will help you be a better counselor:

- *Know your campers.* The more time you take to understand what the campers are like, what they fear, how they learn, what excites them about camp, where they are vulnerable and where they are strong, the better able you will be to connect with them and work with them. Even though you will be working with campers in a group, knowing them as individual young people will greatly enhance your influence with them.

- *Get organized.* Being a counselor can entail a wide variety of tasks and situations, including birthdays, tryouts and activity periods, team or play practice, clean-up jobs, dining hall lists, special diets, and campers who need to get their medication, to name only a few. Add to this mix, taxing emotional elements like, some kids being homesick or being afraid of the dark, and you can have a lot on your plate. Resist the urge to try and carry it "all in your head." Keep a clipboard or notebook with good notes. It is a *job* after all.

- *Smile* a lot, especially when you see each camper for the first time every day. Human beings are "hard-wired" to look at faces. A smile is a universal sign of approachability, acceptance, and friendship. You might actually have to practice this suggestion.

- *Help each camper make a new friend.* If you are doing whatever it takes to help each camper make a new friend at camp, then you are probably already doing a lot right.
- *Ask for help.* I have been treating children and adolescents as a therapist for over 30 years, and I *still* seek out help from those in my field who are more experienced than I am. The day I have nothing new to learn is the day I am kidding myself. As I mentioned in Chapter 2, however, your pride may get in the way of learning or asking for help. Many staff members are afraid to admit that they may not know something or that they're having trouble with a particular camper. None of us wants to look bad, but you will look even worse if you come to the end of a session and have made no progress with certain campers.
- *Admit to two things: what you don't know and your mistakes.* Ironically, children actually admire adults who can be humble. After all, they like it when they aren't the only *learners* in a classroom or at camp. I used to think kids would think less of me if I admitted I didn't know something or if I made a mistake. What I realized is that as long as *my attitude about being a learner was positive and afforded me the opportunity to be wrong or not know,* the kids were just fine with it.
- Remember that *you do not control children so much as you influence them.* It would be nice to think that you could simply impose your authority as a counselor, and your campers would automatically and obediently do as you say. In your dreams! The people most skillful with children are those who know how to *build their influence* with them. Children in the United States have been encouraged to speak up and have their own voice. You will have to *earn* the respect and authority of your campers each and every day.

So, while many counselors would like to think that their work with their campers should all just *come naturally,* the truth is it takes skill, practice, patience, and time. Every year that I return to camp, I learn something new about kids. If you can look at being a camp counselor as a set of skills you can improve on over time and with practice (and did I say patience?), you will do well, not just at camp, but wherever you decide to make your career or life's work.

4

This Sacred Place: Being a Steward for Future Generations

Jupiterimages

Whenever I talk with people who have grown up at camp, I hear remarkable stories about individuals who have made a significant impact on their lives and about the important lessons they have learned there. Counselors who have spent a major part of their childhood at camp have a particular attachment to the place that can border on being possessive. Whenever any significant changes are made to the program or the traditions of their beloved camp, those counselors often react with anger, disbelief, and resistance, as if the place they know so well will somehow be taken away from them or change in a way that will render it unrecognizable. After all, in their experience, this is *their place*—the scene of *their* exciting escapades and *their* growing up. It is as if they are saying, "Don't mess with my childhood!"

To be sure, not all counselors have the same degree of attachment to camp. Those who have grown up at camp will naturally feel more strongly about it than staff members who are about to embark on their first summer there. So, it is a measure of maturity when staff begin to realize how significant camp is in a way that goes beyond any single summer or their own unique experience there. As I said in Chapter 2, what makes camp so great is that it is all about you, and it is not all about you. It is your experience that makes you feel like you own the place and your realization that camp does a lot of good for a lot of people, which will make you want to save and protect it for the future. After all, *generations* of children have gained newfound self-confidence and independence at camp. Many campers have acquired a keen sense of responsibility and accomplishment there. Indeed, camp is a place where *each new, successive generation of children can develop a kind of resilience that comes from being "on their own," away from their parents in a safe, well-monitored experiment in purposeful, cooperative group living.*

The fact that camp can and does have such a tremendous positive impact on young people is what makes me say that camp is a sacred place. Truth be known, most counselors don't think about camp this way. As I have suggested previously, many counselors see camp only through their own personal experience. Yet, camps have been providing this kind of safe learning space for young people for *generations!* Camp is not just for *this summer, but every summer.* In other words, if you truly love the place you call camp, you will want to do everything in your power to preserve its reputation and make sure it is around for years to come. The more you love what camp has done for you, the more you will want to make sure it is there to offer those same benefits to youngsters who have yet to come.

If you behave in a way that compromises the reputation of the camp in the surrounding community or with the current crop of camper families, you aren't just hurting the present day; you are jeopardizing the future. If camp is going to be around next year and the next *20 years,* every adult member of the community needs to see beyond their own experience, profound or meaningful as it may be, and think about how to care for and protect the name and reputation of camp. The group of counselors who goes into town, rents a motel room, and then trashes it in an all-night party isn't thinking about protecting camp. The group of counselors who sneaks into the woods, gets high, and then returns to work with the kids in that altered state isn't thinking about what would happen to the reputation of the place if some kid were to get hurt on their watch. They are just thinking about getting high. Thinking about camp as a sacred space—a perennial scene—where young people get something they can't get most anywhere else is what makes your passion and enthusiasm a mature and positive force.

So, I have a suggestion. Sit down with some of your camp friends, and think out loud about all it has given you: some of your best lifelong friends, as well as some of the best times of your life, where you gained confidence, responsibility, opportunity, adventure, and fun. Share these things in a group, with as many people as can enter the conversation in a serious way. Then, talk about what it would be like if camp didn't exist—if it hadn't been there for you. The true act of mature love for camp is making a commitment to guard, look after, and care for it in a way that will preserve it for time yet to come. Then, go have your fun—in a way that honors and preserves this place for future generations.

5

Famous Presidential Speech Writer Meets Child Therapist: Charity, Clarity, Brevity, Levity

One of the great advantages of living in Boston as I do is having the resources of the John F. Kennedy presidential library about 20 minutes from my house. The library has an ongoing series of visiting speakers who come to talk about both current and historical events. One frequent guest speaker to the library until his death in the fall of 2010 was Ted Sorenson, President Kennedy's speechwriter. The famous and oft-quoted line from Kennedy's inaugural address, "Ask not what your country can do for you; ask what you can do for your country" was only one of many lines Mr. Sorenson wrote for President Kennedy.

At the end of a lecture given at the library by Mr. Sorenson a few years ago, an audience member asked him what he thought the hallmarks of a good speech were. Without hesitating, Mr. Sorenson replied that he thought there were four considerations to writing a good speech. The first, he said, was charity. "Be charitable to your audience" was his advice. He explained that when a speaker acknowledges the contributions, strengths, or positive qualities of the audience, he is not only establishing a rapport and trust with that audience, but is also getting them to listen more intently by complimenting them on the good works they might be doing in their field or in the world at large.

The second consideration, he continued, was clarity. Say what you want to say in simple, accessible, and clear terms. He said the best speeches were those where the messages were clear and directly stated. Being clear with your audience assured that they would walk out of the address with a few well-articulated ideas they could hold onto. The clearer the message, the more likely its chances of being put into practice. As Mr. Sorenson pointed out, a good speech can be entertaining, but to be truly great—to have impact—it had to be memorable. Making your points in a lucid, easily understood manner was one way to produce that effect.

The third quality of a great speech, he contended, was brevity. Audiences, like people in general, he said, appreciate it when you respect their time. Once you have made your points, honor your audience by ending your talk. Doing so allows them to absorb and integrate what it is they have just heard. If you continue to talk, your audience will be forced to listen rather than digest what you have said, making it less likely that they will integrate it into their thinking. Taking up too much time creates resentment in your audience, which might undo any good your speech might otherwise have accomplished. When a reporter remarked to Lincoln about how brief his address at Gettysburg had been, he famously replied, "Had I more time, I would have made it even shorter." All good speakers and speechwriters, Mr. Sorenson asserted, know that it is much harder to say something in concise terms than it is to go on and on. "Don't wear out your audience. If you do, you reduce your impact."

The final characteristic of a great speech is levity. Expressing something with humor is like eating sugar to help the medicine go down. People respond to humor not only because it is stimulating and entertaining, but because it also aids in the consideration of serious issues. A lighthearted approach delivered with skill allows us to keep issues of gravity in better perspective.

When I heard Mr. Sorenson say these things, which he undoubtedly did with greater clarity, brevity, and levity than I have in rendering them here, I immediately thought, "These are also the characteristics of great communication with children. I just never put it in such clear terms: charity, clarity, brevity, levity." I will explain.

When I speak with a child, especially when I want to get them to listen with greater intent, I start with charity. That is, I *validate* them. I talk about or point out a strength or a positive intention of theirs or frame things in such a way as to understand why they may have been tempted by something or drawn to something, even though that "something" may have just gotten them into trouble. Being "charitable" with a child communicates *my* positive intention: that I am not here to shame or judge them, but to understand them and help them *change their behavior*. It is a way of establishing safety and trust in the relationship. Without a positive or charitable approach, children are less likely to open up to you. For whatever else we might say about parents today, most parents do a pretty good job of being charitable with their children.

Being charitable is not the same thing as being permissive, however. I am still going to hold a child accountable for what they may have done or make my point about what is appropriate or expected behavior directly, but that is where clarity comes in.

When it comes to clarity, children actually appreciate it when we get right to the point. Saying things clearly to a child also means using language they can easily grasp. Saying things in "adult-speak" (that is, using words that are more complicated than they need to be or language that is vague and rambling) only makes a child feel confused, shamed, or inadequate. It also risks that *the child never actually truly comprehends what it is you are trying to get across to them.* If we use language that makes *us* feel good but never actually gets the point across, then what have we accomplished? Clarity also requires that we *take a clear stand* on an issue and place a demand or limit on a child. While some parents today may be good at the "charity" piece, they are not always as good about being firm and clear with their children.

Then, there is brevity. Can you ever remember a time when you had done something wrong as a child and an adult went on and on in their lecture to you, even though you got the "message" after the first two minutes? I think everyone has a story like that. The following three key points can be made about being brief in our communication with children today:

1) Once children "get" what we are trying to say, if we continue to talk, *we are actually impeding or interrupting* them from *assimilating the insight or line of reasoning we have just shared with them.* The human brain cannot consciously attend to more than one thing at a time. By making children listen to us go on and on, we are *preventing them* from mulling over or *internalizing* what we have just said. It's one or the other—they can't do both at the same time!

2) Once we have made our point plain, belaboring our message may make *us* feel better, but it then becomes a way of humiliating and belittling the child. Creating such feelings in a child may do a great job of making them feel resentful (and in

turn, less compliant), but it probably actually works *against* any hope of them actually taking in what we are saying. We have to make a decision: Is our intention to make a child feel bad or change their behavior?

3) Because of the popularity of texting, instant messaging, Twitter®, e-mail, and other virtual and electronic forms of communication, children are used to picking up critical bits of information in very short bits. They may actually be better at teasing out the essential part of what we are saying than we are in saying it. "Brief" is the hallmark of modern communication.

Being brief does not mean we can't be thorough. It simply means getting to the point quickly and then ending for maximum impact.

Levity, or the ability to keep things light, is a quality that I use to different degrees, depending on the situation. Obviously, if I am speaking with a child about a very serious incident, I am sober in my tone of voice in order to match the gravity of the situation. Overall, however, my intention is to *change behavior.* Keeping things "light" can mean more than just being humorous. It means being positive, optimistic, or upbeat about a child's *ability to change.* "I know you can do this" is an example of levity. Recent brain research tells us that when we are positive with children, we are more likely to get a positive response from them in return. If our intention is to motivate children to change for the better, then *being positive with them about their ability to change* is critical.

Let me demonstrate how these qualities might show up in a conversation with a camper. A few years ago, while visiting a coed resident camp in the Pocono Mountain region of Pennsylvania, I heard about a 12-year-old boy who had a severe temper problem. "James" had been a camper for several years and had a reputation for getting very angry when things didn't go his way. His temper seemed mostly to flare up in one of two places: in the cabin, when he somehow felt slighted by another camper, or at an activity area, when a play or judgment didn't work out in his favor. I conferred with his counselor, Mike, and with his unit director, and then I met with James and his counselor. The following is part of the conversation I had with the boy, which I will use to demonstrate the four Sorenson principles in action.

Bob (facing the counselor first, speaking calmly, but enthusiastically): Hey, Mike, how's it goin'? Good to see you again. (I smile and "high-five" the counselor so the camper can clearly see my positive, upbeat mood. By doing this, I am conveying *charity* and *levity* in an action form. I want to suggest to the camper my positive intentions). And you must be James. Hey, James! (I extend my hand and smile—again, *charity* and *levity* in a non-verbal form.)

(I direct the camper and counselor on where to sit, placing the boy between his counselor and me.)

Bob (after explaining who I am): So, James, you're not in trouble or anything. Mike and I just wanted to sit down with you and see how camp was going for you. Just how long have you been coming to camp, James?

James: This is my fourth summer.

Bob: Wow! So, you're a real veteran. You must be an expert about this place. (*Charity:* I am *validating* James's experience here as an experienced camper.)

Bob (continuing): So, Mike here (turning to face the boy's counselor) has been telling me that you can be a real help in the cabin sometimes. Mike, didn't you tell me James sometimes offers to help you clean up the area outside the cabin, even when it's not his job? (Charity: I am again validating a specific positive behavior James has been known to show.)

Mike: That's right, Bob. And the other day when one of the new kids, Zack, was having trouble finding his baseball glove in the cabin, James offered to help him.

Bob: Yeah, I remember you told me about that. (Turning my gaze from Mike back to James, I continue.) And Mike also told me that one of the things you seem to like the most at camp is tennis. Is that right, James?

James: Yeah, that's right.

Bob: So, one of the other things Mike told me, James, is that from time to time you've volunteered to stay after and help pick up some of the stray tennis balls that have been hit out of the courts. (*Charity:* I am *validating* James's helpfulness down at tennis.)

Mike: Yeah, that's true, Bob. James has also sometimes helped show some of the newer players a few tips about their grip. He can really be pretty helpful to the tennis instructor. (Mike chimes in with another example of *charity,* again *validating* James's occasional helpfulness at tennis.)

Bob: So, I don't know, James, if you knew that Mike, here, was bragging about you like this, but he's had some pretty positive things to say about you.

He also told me that there are times, either down at tennis or at another activity or in the cabin, when you have lost your temper. He says sometimes you can get so mad—so upset—that it's hard for you let anyone help you with whatever might be going on. (Clarity: a clear, straightforward statement of the fact of his temper.) Is that true?

James: Yeah, I guess so.

Bob: So, the reason Mike brought you to talk with me is not because you're in trouble right now, but because he wants to try to help you. And I'm glad he did, because you know what I think? I think *you don't like it* when you lose your temper. And let me tell you why. (This approach is *charity* and *clarity* working together with a lighthearted approach, or *levity.*)

First, if you keep losing your temper, I'm afraid some of the other kids might start to get the wrong idea about you. They're going to start to think you're a hothead. They might even start to tease you about it just to see if they can set you off. Because when you do lose your temper, they're not the ones who get into trouble; *you are.* What's worse, we know you can be a really nice guy, and yet, you're probably going to start to get a bad "rep" from some of the other guys. And when you do lose your temper, you end up having to come talk to people like me, and we know *that's* not fun! (*Levity* again.)

It seems to me, James, that it's like that temper of yours gets the best of you—like it's running you, rather than you being in charge of it. So, Mike and I want to help you with it. (This point is cutting right to the chase, or solution, and is an example of *brevity.*)

* * * * *

From here, I quickly help Mike and James develop a plan that involves James having a "cooling off spot," where he can go when he's getting upset, which will help him "catch" himself before he actually blows his top. I also have Mike and James develop a "secret signal" that either can use when Mike thinks James needs to go cool off or James thinks he needs to go cool off.

Once we had the problem stated clearly, no reason existed to belabor it. This boy is an individual who is caught in a bad habit that he doesn't know how to change. Sermonizing, moralizing, or expressing our frustration with him might make *us* feel better, but it isn't going to help this boy do what we say we want him to do—namely, change his behavior and control his temper. (*Brevity* in action.)

The use of cooling off spots and secret signals are both examples of skills that are further discussed in greater detail in Chapter 7.

6

One-on-One Basic Communication Skills With Campers

Jupiterimages

Everyone who works with children should know about and master a number of basic communication and interactive skills, including the 33 skills detailed in this chapter. These techniques are the building blocks of creating trust, establishing a strong positive connection, and working on conflicts with children. This chapter features a brief overview of each of the different basic skills or strategies. You need to master these basic skills before moving on to the more advanced skills or strategies outlined in Chapter 7.

Embedded in this set of basic skills are four or so of the more common mistakes that most adults make with children, for example:

Key point #13: Drop the rope—a master skill. (Avoiding power struggles.)

Key point #14: State what you expect in positive terms.

Key point #25: Less is more. (We talk too much and lose kids in the process.)

Key point #26: We get too emotional (and blur our impact in the process).

Before you look at the skills themselves, let me first say a word about technique. Kids know when they're being "techniqued." In other words, unless you truly adopt these skills as your own and integrate them into your natural repertoire, you will seem fake to kids. The overriding principal of working with anyone—children, parents, colleagues, or friends—is to be truly present. If you are simply going through the motions or doing something because you heard it was a good way to get kids to do what you want them to do, you will come off as inauthentic and untrustworthy. Learning the skills or techniques presented in this book means internalizing them, so they become a part of your natural way of talking and acting. It's part of getting "Ditter-ized!"

Key point #1:
Be aware that nonverbal communication counts.

Ever find yourself humming a tune you can't identify, even though it's maddeningly familiar? If you're like most people, it probably drives you a little crazy. It's interesting how a tune can get our attention from out of nowhere. I often wonder how long the tune has been on my mind before I actually noticed it.

That's exactly what the nonverbal part of communication does: it gets into our heads and helps form an impression almost without us "knowing." When we say we have a "feeling" about someone, often that "feeling" or impression comes from some nonverbal communication our senses are taking in, even though we may not always be aware of it.

For example, songs have what I call the "words and the music." The tune, or "music," is recognized by a part of the brain that is entirely separate from the part that identifies the words—just as the part of the brain that recognizes what someone says is very different from the part that "reads" their body language—or the way they say it.

Nonverbal communication, for example, the look on your face, the tone in your voice, the way you say something, how you stand or move, whether you are flushed or calm, is often more meaningful to children than what you actually say. Kids pick up on our "hidden operating system" or nonverbal language, and determine whether we are safe or "cool," simply by reading the look on our face or the tone in our voice. In fact, school-aged children "get" about 70 percent of their communication from others nonverbally, while four to six year-olds get up to 80 percent of the meaning from others nonverbally. (It is interesting that many children like popular songs for the music and don't become aware of the words until they are much older.)

People who are very effective with children are very aware of their nonverbal communication, as well as that of the children or people with whom they work. This factor is one of the most fundamental areas of skill that anyone can have working with children. The more aware you are of the nonverbal language of yourself and others, the more effective you will be with people—particularly with children.

Key point #2: Make eye contact.

One of the most fundamental aspects of communicating with children is making eye contact with them. In fact, the brain has several different parts that tune into the human face, noting the nuances of a look we may be getting from someone else. About two to six weeks after an infant is born, when they can actually focus on an object and "see" it, they begin to make serious eye contact with their primary caretakers, smiling excitedly when their eyes meet up.

It is clearly a sign of progress when a child you don't know can hold your gaze and not look away. I would say that unwavering, clear eye contact is as solid a measure of trust as any other gesture you can make.

If you read Chapter 1, you know that children today spend a lot of time looking at screens—television screens, computer screens, cell phone screens, and video game screens. What this factor means is that children have learned how to appear like they are paying attention and taking in what you are communicating with them about, although they may actually be distracted. Getting a child to hold your non-threatening gaze is one way to increase the chances that they are actually listening to you.

That said, some children are clearly listening, even though they are not looking you in the eye. That's because some children have been taught to look down when an adult speaks to them as a sign of respect. Also, when children are feeling shamed, they will often look away, even though they are listening to what you are saying. This response is simply a face-saving device. Depriving a child of this way of holding onto their dignity by forcing them to look you in the eyes might make you feel better, but it will probably actually reduce the probability the child hears you and takes in what you say. Once a child is experiencing a certain amount of shame, it will prevent them from absorbing the lesson or understanding you are trying to pass on.

Jupiterimages

Key point #3: Smile!

Customer service personnel and companies that spend a lot of time dealing with the public spend thousands of dollars undergoing professional training in which one of the essential messages is simply, "smile!"

So many parts of the human brain are designed to have us focus on and decipher the human face and all of its nuances and expressions that it is hard to miss how important it is simply to smile. Universally recognized as an offering of warmth, friendship, and trust, a smile invites others to engage with us. Yet, it is amazing how frequently we don't smile, especially when we spend a lot of time with the same people in a day, like at summer camp. Smiling is the best way to build rapport with a child. Whatever mood you may be in personally, by smiling when you see a child, you immediately communicate two things: first, that you are delighted in the presence of that child; and second, that you are willing to put your own preoccupations aside temporarily and truly be present and in the moment with them.

Powerful stuff! This factor is especially powerful when you consider that many parents today are looking at a PDA of some kind when they are with their children.

If, the first time you see each camper every day, you were to make an effort to give them a big smile, it might make all the difference in the world in you being able to form a strong positive relationship with them.

Jupiterimages

Key point #4: Be on the same physical level.

Some skills or ways of being with children aren't used all the time. Being on the same physical level is one of them. However, it's handy to have this maneuver in your "bag of tricks," even if you ultimately decide not to use it in any given situation.

Adults are usually taller than the children with whom they work. Children are used to looking up at us. It is a rare moment when a child and an adult are on the same physical level and can actually look each other directly in the eye. It's a moment that stands out as special and unusual for children, which is why it makes an impact on some of them.

When I want to make a special point about something or when I feel the situation calls for me to make a stronger level of contact with a child, I do one of the following, depending on the situation:

- Kneel down next to younger children (this technique is the most dramatic move).
- Sit next to or across from slightly older children (while this positioning is less dramatic, it can create great impact).
- Stand with teens, with my legs apart in such a way that I lower myself to their height (this adjustment is a subtle maneuver).

David De Lossy

Key point #5: Know the "three safe places" to touch a child—the advantages of light physical touch.

If you have ever seen any of my training videos or DVDs, you have probably heard me talk about the "three safe places" to touch a child. Before I go into what those places are, let me initially detail the advantage of using light, non-threatening physical contact with campers.

First, if a child is distracted, either by something inside their head or in the outside environment, they often can't hear you when you're talking to them. The more distracted they are, the less able they are to "hear" you. Putting a hand on their shoulder or the side of their arm gets their attention and helps you hold it, along with your direct eye contact, until you can get your message across. (Remember brevity. Get to your point quickly.)

If a child is down at the pool, for example, and is excited about swimming, nervous about changing, and stimulated by the splashing and the reflection of light on the water, it is understandable that they might not hear you when you tell them to got to the sunscreen station and get sunscreen on—or whatever your particular message might be.

As such, a light hand on their upper arm, shoulder, or upper back will help get their attention, focus them briefly, and even steady or calm them. In this regard, the following pointers can be helpful:

- Little kids—and in this instance, I mean up to age six or seven, you can take by the hand. Take the hand of a 10- or 12-year-old and they think it's weird—and they're right.
- If you approach a younger child, say under the age of eight, in a way that they are surprised by you ("blindsided," so to speak), any advantage of the light physical touch will undoubtedly be lost by their having been startled.
- If a child pulls away or is noticeably uncomfortable with being touched, simply respect their personal space, without bringing a lot of attention to it, and drop your hand.
- Many guys think that one of the three safe places to touch a boy is on the head. Unless you know the youngster personally and very well, I would stay away from patting a kid on the head. It can sometimes have the effect of being condescending to that child.
- Like any other skill, the more you become comfortable with it yourself, the more natural and useful it will feel. Using light physical touch to enhance a connection or deepen the listening or holding the attention or calming a child can be very effective, if you use it with care.
- In no instance, should anyone touch a child on his or her upper thighs or in a place that would normally be covered by their bathing suit. If a child has a rash, a cut, or a problem, get a health care professional and have another adult present if you need to look at that area of a child's body for health purposes.

Key point #6: Develop a "look" of your own.

In the first part of this chapter, nonverbal communication and the importance of eye contact were discussed. I talked about how you could get a "feeling" about someone just by the things your senses might be taking in—a look on their face, a tone in their voice, and so on. A prime example of the power of nonverbal communication comes from your own parents. If you are like most people, one or both of your parents had what I call "the look." That is, when they were not happy about something you had done, they simply gave you a stern "look," which made it very clear that they were seriously upset with you, without them ever having to say a word. In my own case, when my mother was unhappy with me, the look was really all I needed to immediately feel regret for whatever it was I had done to put that look on her face.

If you as a counselor don't have a "look" of your own, you had better develop one before the campers arrive. What I mean by a look, however, is not necessarily threatening or mean-spirited. The "look" I am talking about is simply a quiet, calm, steady, non-smiling gaze that says, "This is not funny. This is serious."

The idea behind having such a "look" is actually to get you as a caretaker to slow down and focus in with a child and be in a serious frame of mind. It doesn't need to be punitive—just clear: "this is important." You might accompany your "look" with the words, "I know you probably didn't mean anything by it, but we don't do that here." Or simply with the utterance, "No."

Key point #7: Develop a second "look"—praise.

Having a serious, calm, but focused and sober, "look" as detailed in the previous point is more effective when you can counterbalance it with a look that is more praising and positive. Much like a smile, catching kids in the act of doing something right can help you establish a trusting relationship with your campers. That said, the following specific points about praise can be made:

- If you praise kids for the everyday, ordinary things that they are expected to do, and they won't trust the praise or you. When we praise kids for things that they should be doing anyway, they actually distrust us, because they think we are only trying to make them feel better.
- Accordingly, campers should only be praised for things that they have truly earned or worked hard on.
- If a child has done a poor job and an adult praises her anyway, the child doesn't trust the praise or the adult who is passing it out.
- When praising a child, it is critical to praise them for how they did something or for a detail, rather than just the final product. When a child hears, "Oh, that was the best picture," they are skeptical. Talking about the use of color or how they shaded something or how well they drew a particular object is more meaningful and believable.
- Acknowledging when a camper helps another camper ("That was great the way you helped Sally look for her lost tennis racquet this morning"); does something extra during clean-up ("Thanks for picking up all the trash outside the cabin. It really looks great!"); or has improved on a particular task ("You got your laundry into your laundry bag today without me asking. That's great!") can make an especially positive impression on a camper and her group. A more expansive overview of how to use public appreciation, or group praise, in a very specific and beneficial way is included in the next chapter (key point #39).

Key point #8: A word about praising teens.

If you praise a 9- or 10-year-old by telling them how proud you are of them, most of them will likely beam with delight. On the other hand, if you tell a teenager how proud you are of them, they will probably gag. Any language we use with teenagers that makes them feel small (e.g., that draws attention to the fact that they are dependent on us in any way) will backfire. This situation occurs because teens are constantly trying to act as if they don't count on us for validation or for anything else for that matter. To admit that they needed something from us would feel make them poor and needy.

One of the main developmental tasks of adolescents is to develop their own identity and sense of self. The reason teens often push back against their parents is because they are trying to establish their own personality as separate from their parents. As I sometimes say to adolescents in my therapy practice, "Maybe someday it won't bother you so much that you're a little like your mother in this way!"

So, how do you praise adolescents? Tell them how impressed you are with whatever they've accomplished. When we tell someone we are impressed, we are inferring that they are more our equals, rather than insinuating that we are in a position above them and thus qualified to judge them. All of this message gets communicated in just a simple phrase. To say we are impressed is like honoring their individuality, without making them feel small and dependent.

Hemera/Thinkstock

Key point #9: You have two relationships with teenagers.

Another basic principle of working with adolescents is the understanding that as an adult leader, you always have two relationships with them. The first is your more private, off-to-the-side relationship with each one, where you can speak about more personal matters without embarrassing them in front of their peers. One of the critical things to understand about teens is that they would rather do just about anything, including take high personal risks or get into trouble with an adult authority, than look bad in front of their peers. Anyone working with teens who violates this central principle and says or does something to humiliate them in front of their peers has just done serious damage to their relationship with that individual, to say nothing of creating a poor impression with the rest of the group by appearing non-trustworthy. After all, if you embarrass one teen in front of his or her friends, what's to say you won't do it again with someone else in the group?

The other relationship you have with an adolescent is the one you have with them when they are with their friends. In this scenario, you cannot draw attention to any way that one of the members might count on or depend on you. Remember, teens are all about appearing grown up and independent, whether they truly are or not. If you violate that "teen code," you risk being rejected by the group.

Thinkstock Images

Key point #10: Learn about each camper.

As has already been discussed, we do not control kids so much as we influence them. We do not influence kids if they don't feel we truly know them. In some cases, children come to camp from a home life where they have not only one or more teachers in school, but perhaps an after-school care provider, a tutor, a music instructor, a coach, and maybe even a speech, mental health, or behavioral therapist. To them, you are just one more adult passing through their life. Why would they want to listen to you and do what you ask them if you are just one more adult?

The time you take to truly get to know your kids—to enter their "reality"—is critical, if you want to have any influence with them. What kind of music do they listen to? What are their favorite TV shows? What movies have they seen? For most kids, regardless of their age, if they have a pet and you take an interest in that, you have just taken one more step toward bonding with that child. What do they like doing at camp the most? The least? What do they think about global warming or saving the environment or other issues?

It is not just what you share in your conversation, but the time you spend with them that makes an impact. Play with your kids. Get in the pool with them, and let them chase you or splash you. Play cards at rest hour with them. Bake cookies together, or get on the ropes course with them. Talk with them about issues they find important in the world. In focus groups, I helped lead with over 2,000 campers in six cities across the United States several years ago, when we asked the campers what it was that their favorite counselors did that made them their favorite counselors, time and time again the children said that their favorite counselors were those who spent time with us even, when they didn't have to. Remember, your greatest asset in working with children in any setting, and certainly at camp, is the relationship you build with them.

iStockphoto/Thinkstock

Key point #11: Encourage new friendships.

One of the things that most kids point to when they talk about what they like most about camp are the friends they make there. For some children, making friends is easy. For whatever reason, they are relaxed, calm, and confident when they find themselves in a group of new kids. For other children, the task is more daunting. Some children sit back and watch for a while before jumping into the fray. Others have an easier time making friends, when the group size is smaller or when they are doing something they feel confident about.

A great focus for you as a counselor is to do a mental "survey" of the friendships in your cabin or group (a process I refer to as "mapping a group," which you can actually chart on paper if you want). Subsequently, by looking at the "map of friendships" in your cabin or group, you can more easily identify who might need help making a new friend. When you take the time to help two kids get to know one another, perhaps by asking them to join in playing a game or doing an activity with you, you are simply helping facilitate a process that is natural and just may need a little boost to get started.

Mapping your group has other benefits as well. You can often see how kids will feel left out or how they may compete with one another for attention or status in the group. You may even see where potential rivalries or bullying problems might arise. The more you are aware of how your campers are doing, the better chance you have of helping them get the most out of their time at camp. Chapter 9 provides additional information on the steps involved in "mapping a group."

Stockbyte

Key point #12: Move toward your campers.

When you are in a cabin, tent, or room, and you want to get the attention of a particular camper, if you are like most counselors, you simply shout out something. A more effective technique is to use the camper's name and move in their direction. Using their name and moving toward them creates momentum and adds weight to getting and holding their attention.

The one exception to this point is when you are at an activity area with a large group of campers, and one or two are not paying attention. In this instance, what some leaders do is to keep talking, while working their way over to the offending campers, thus moving quietly in their direction in such a way as to subtly, but effectively, draw attention to the fact that they are distracting from the group. Other activity leaders simply and suddenly stop talking, which immediately draws attention to the kids who are talking.

Hemera/Thinkstock

Key point #13: Drop the rope—a master skill.

I have a story I tell counselors, teachers and parents—and any adults who work with children. The focus of the tale is that every child has a "rope," or more precisely, an invisible "fishing line" that they carry at all times. These fishing lines are given out to every child throughout the world at birth. When children come to camp they "pack them up" and bring them along in their "emotional duffel bag."

Campers use these "fishing lines", of course, to go fishing. Except they aren't fishing for fish; they're fishing for you, their counselor. And how do they do this? They "throw out their line" by provoking you into a power struggle. Some kids do this by ignoring you. Others do it by challenging you. Since 1997, when the TV show *South Park* made its debut, children have flatly challenged adults by saying to them, "You're not the boss of me!" This declaration, first uttered by Eric, Kyle, and Stan, the kids in *South Park,* is a child's way of "throwing you their line," hoping that you will pick it up and engage in the battle. They love it when you do. Why? Because as long as children get us, as adults, to argue with them, they not only feel empowered ("look at what I've gotten this big adult to do"), but they also get to put off doing whatever it is they should be doing by spending that time arguing with you.

Youngsters use several "lines" to "hook" us into a power struggle or tug-of-war. One predictable line is the "I-hope-you-know-this-is-a-free-country" statement, implying that they can do whatever they want. Or the "my parents paid a lot of money for me to come to this camp! I can do what I want!" Or the even more galling assertion, "My parents paid for me to come here. In fact, I pay your salary! You work for me! You make my bed!" That's when you can imagine taking that fishing line and doing something really creative with it.

When a child draws us into a power struggle, often our first impulse is to engage. I call that engagement picking up the rope. In reality, if you want to be more effective with children in general, let alone at camp, your first strategy should be to drop the rope. By that I don't mean that we let kids do whatever they want. I mean avoiding the power struggle as much as you can. The following steps are involved in "dropping the rope:"

- Stay calm. The reason a child is provocative with you in the first place is to unbalance and unnerve you. As soon as you lose your cool, you have picked up the rope. And they win; you lose.
- Make kids "right" about that part of what they are saying that is technically correct. For example, I would say, "You're right. I'm not your parent." Or, "You're right. I'm not the boss of you." Or I might say, "You're right. It is a free country. Isn't that great!" Or I could say, "I'm glad your parents could afford to send you here. This is a great place!" Whatever you say, you must say it calmly and without sarcasm.
- When a child is expecting to trip you up, get you to lose your cool, and have a gut reaction to their provocation, and you don't, you are actually winning the battle of wits. They hate that! It's like being really angry about a service or product you felt

wronged by and the person you want to pick a fight with—some poor, unsuspecting service person—is really nice. They're so agreeable and helpful that you just want to scream. But you can't. They hold the power by being calm and exerting great self-control.

- After you "make a kid right about what he is right about," you should pause. Let that sink in. While you might only pause for a fraction of a second, pausing will hold their attention for that moment, which enables you to secure your grip on the command of the interaction. Then simply say, "And…" Most people say… "but…," which is a mistake. Saying "but" negates everything you just said before. "But" is also a word all children are programmed to tune out when they hear any adult utter it. Say, "And…"

- At this point, being as casually deliberate as you can, state what you expect or what is true for camp. For example, "You're right. I'm not your parent. (Pause.) And… everybody knows that when you come to camp, you help clean up." Or, "I'm glad your parents could afford to send you here. This is a great place. (Pause.) And… they didn't send you here to be wild." Or, "And…helping out is part of camp." By speaking in this way you, are practicing clarity.

- Then practice brevity and levity, and move on. One of the things most adults do is to stay locked in with a child. While times may exist when a safety issue may make it impossible to move on, in most instances, once you've said your piece, moving your attention to the next camper or next activity forces the child to face a sobering choice: either move along or take this to the next level. To be sure, some kids will go to the next level. In my experience, more than 85 percent of kids drop the issue.

Picking up the rope, or engaging a child in a power struggle, is a mistake I see most parents, teachers, and camp counselors make. Most counselors tell me that this skill is the number one practice they use more than any other procedure during the summer.

Hemera/Thinkstock

Key point #14: State what you expect in positive terms (the brain can't hold a negative).

Another common mistake many people working with children make is to tell children what they don't want them to do rather than what they do want them to do. Problems will exist with this approach, not the least of which is the fact that our brains can't hold a negative. For example, if you tell kids at the pool or waterfront, "Hey, don't run," their brain hears "run!" If you say, "Don't talk while I'm talking," the child can't help but hear, "Talk while I'm talking!" I don't know anything that we can tell a child not to do where we don't simultaneously suggest the very thing we are asking them to stop.

On occasion, a child may respond appropriately when you tell them what you don't want them to do. But they won't be able to keep from doing it for too long. What takes more thinking and effort is to tell a child what we do want them to do, in other words, to tell campers in positive terms what we expect, for example, "Walk;" "Wait until I'm finished, then you can raise your hand and speak;" "Keep your hands to yourself."

It turns out that children are less likely to stop doing something that is unwanted or inappropriate unless we give them an idea of something else to do in the place of that behavior. Chapter 10 provides an overview of the steps involved in establishing "agreements" with campers. This chapter details more information about how giving children something to do that replaces what we don't want them to do is a critical factor in changing their behavior.

Hemera/Thinkstock

Key point #15: Thank younger kids first for doing what you ask them to do.

When you are working with children between the ages of four and eight or nine, always thank them first for doing what you are about to ask them to do. For example, "Thank you, Sally, for waiting until I say you can go." "Thank you, Joseph, for sitting quietly with your hands to yourself while we are sitting in the meeting."

For this approach to work, your tone of voice needs to be sincere, not sarcastic. When a child that age hears us being grateful and nice to them about something they haven't yet done, they feel more inclined to do it. It's almost as if their line of thinking is, "Well, I guess I should do it since they've already thanked me for it." Obviously, an older child would scoff at us if we tried this technique with them. The key, however, is the positive tone in our voice, which most children hear as inviting. It is as if they feel complimented and therefore compelled to return the favor by obliging.

Stockbyte

Key point #16: State what you expect, and detach.

Although this point was previously addressed in the section on dropping the rope, it is so useful with teens that it deserves a section all its own. Teenagers have a particular talent for arguing adults under the table. As I have often said jokingly, everyone knows that all American children have been to law school by age four. Furthermore, adolescents have an uncanny way of resembling four-year-olds.

When setting a limit with an adolescent, it is much more effective to state what you expect, in positive terms, and detach. To a teenager who is protesting going to an activity, you might say, "Look, I know you don't like soccer, so I'm not going to make you play. You need to be there with the rest of the kids, however, until we can get something else worked out. So, I expect to see you down there in five minutes!"

A typical teenager won't be there in five minutes. They will be there in nine minutes, just to make a point (the point being that they are still their own person and not really listening to you). I call this being within "the spirit of the law," and I wouldn't make a battle out of it (refer to the next point on "picking your battles").

Again, about 85 percent of campers comply. For those who don't, point #34 (the "respect" conversation and point #33 (ask for help) can provide you with additional guidance.

iStockphoto/Thinkstock

Key point #17: Pick your battles.

In the previous point, "state your expectations and detach," an example was detailed of how a teenager will often be a few minutes late just to express or convey their independence. Many adults make the mistake of getting into a battle with a teen about those few minutes. With all children, but with teens in particular, it is important to understand what I call the "spirit of the law." In other words, when an adolescent complies within reason and, in the example of the activity period, comes just a few minutes late, you would do well to focus on the fact that they showed up. Obviously, showing up for only the last few minutes of an activity period is not within the spirit of the law. If that occurred, you should do a "walk and talk" (refer to point #30) or address it off to the side, when you have your first chance.

Another example is cleanup. If you are looking to bounce a quarter off the bed of a teen or eat off the floor after they have just swept it, maybe you should be at West Point and not camp. By picking battles over exactitude, you are creating what teens see as a hostile environment that makes them feel subordinate. Again, great for Parris Island, but not for a children's summer camp.

That said, some things at camp, like any place, are simply non-negotiable. These factors are the sorts of issues on which you, as a counselor, need to stand firm. Most of these points are safety matters. For example, everyone has to wear a seat belt when in a camp vehicle. Everyone has to wear a personal floatation device (PFD) when they take a sailboat, canoe, or water bike out on the lake. When it comes to physical or emotional safety, we don't compromise. Indeed, as the counselor and the adult, you are the person on the front line whose job it is to safeguard the campers in your charge. The mental, physical, and emotional "space" or environment that you maintain and in which your campers thrive is what I call the "envelope of safety." In this instance, you are expected to pick your battles and protect your "envelope of safety."

Comstock

Key point #18: Take kids aside.

When a camper is either being defiant or somehow signaling that they need more attention than you may have given them thus far, the best move is to take kids aside. Two reasons exist for taking campers aside. The first is simply that facing them one-on-one offers fewer distractions to both you and the camper. The other is that whatever you have to say to that camper will be less embarrassing to them if you do it away from their peers. Keep in mind my previous point about kids wanting to avoid being humiliated in front of their peers at all costs. Once you have embarrassed a child in front of others, it is difficult to regain their trust or establish a positive working relationship with them.

Taking a camper aside might mean going out on the porch of a cabin, stepping just outside the dining hall, or walking a few feet away from and out of ear shot of the rest of the group. Times will exist when taking a camper aside will actually grab the attention of the other campers. In that case, you have to make a judgment call. Is it best to go ahead and separate that camper at the risk of the other campers seeing the situation unfold and reacting negatively to it; or is better to wait for another opportunity, when you will have more privacy? Point #34, "respect conversation," in the next chapter, provides additional information on the value of taking kids aside.

Marilyn Barbone

Key point #19: Separate the "player" from the "audience."

When a camper is acting up, being defiant, or distracting the other campers from doing what they are supposed to be doing, a key strategy is to remove that camper, or "player," from their audience. This point is the cousin to the previous point (#18). You can accomplish this separation either by having your co-counselor take the rest of the group and going ahead to another location while you stay behind with the camper, or by going with that camper away from the group. The point in this instance is that in addition to risking that the camper might be humiliated by the confrontation with you, I find that kids often like to "play" to the audience. For example, they love the attention or the laughs or encouragement they may be getting from the group and "play" off that attention by being provocative with you. As such, an audience can also embolden bad behavior. The adrenalin/dopamine rush causes some kids to become disinhibited, which is a fancy way of saying they can become more impulsive. Removing the camper from the audience or the audience from the camper can help the disruptive individual calm down and regain their composure. With the other kids temporarily not around, it also gives you more of a chance to regain the defiant camper's undivided attention.

Key point #20: Get Onboard. Join with campers first.

Let's say you walk into cabin cleanup, and the kids are playing a spirited game of hockey with a small ball and brooms, rather than cleaning. You could either yell at them or join in the game for a minute, as a way of joining with the campers. You could then get them to redirect their energies to cleaning up. (For more information on "redirecting behavior," see refer to point #27.)

Or, let's say you come across a child sitting on her bed looking at a picture album or listening to her i-Pod®. Again, you could scold or chide the camper for not making her bed, or you could take two minutes and sit down with her to see what she is looking at or listening to and engage her in a conversation. After connecting with her, which would probably take only a few moments of your time, you would tell her how great it was to share her pictures or music and then turn her attention to making her bed. You can always tell her that you'd love to talk more after she's finished. It might sound like the following:

Wow, Rachel, this is a great photo album. Thanks for sharing it with me. Maybe, we can look at it some more during rest hour. But, you know what I need from you right now? I need you to help clean up. Can you help me with that? And if there's anything you need me to help you with, let me know. Thanks, Rachel.

The aforementioned are examples of joining with campers. Like I said previously, children often don't have any reason to invest in you as just another transient adult in their life. Taking time to actually connect with them tells a child that you are interested in them as a person and not just in them as a job that needs to get done.

Jupiterimages

Key point #21: Offer limited choice.

One thing that has changed dramatically in the last several years is the sheer amount of choice that children have been given in many aspects of their lives. When I grew up, there were three channels on television: ABC, CBS, and NBC. Today, some cable companies offer well over 200 different channels. When I grew up, a house had one landline telephone, often shared on what was called a "party line" with another household or two. Today, everyone has their own cell or "smart" phone, which itself offers several ways of communicating: texting, e-mail, Twitter®, Facebook®, or some other social networking site; or actually calling someone. (In reality, most teens use their cell phones as phones less than 30 percent of the time.)

The point is that children today are used to having a lot of choices. Not all of that choice is such a good thing. In some instances, the brain of a child isn't really prepared to deal with so much choice. Having certainty and more structure, which is to say, having more specific and clearer expectations and fewer choices, can be a relief to many children. The problem is that children have become accustomed to being given more choices. One example is food. "Do you want a chicken leg, pasta, salad, or a hamburger?" I once heard a mother say to her four-year-old. As the child became more agitated (from being more overwhelmed by so many choices), the mother, in desperation, kept adding even more choices.

With your campers, I would offer what I call limited choice. For example, during cabin cleanup, I might ask a child what they would like to do first: make their bed, put their dirty laundry away, or sweep under their bed? Just a few tasks, all of which have to get done, but giving the child the power to choose gives them some sense of control over their world.

Jupiterimages

Key point #22: One thing at a time, three at the most

The previous point detailed giving a limited number of choices to children because it is less overwhelming, while still allowing them some say in making decisions about their life at camp. When you are working with younger children or children of any age who have attention deficit disorder, it is best to give no more than three directions at a time. The reason for this guideline is that once you go past three things, kids start forgetting what the first thing was you said.

"We're going down to the waterfront. You need a towel, sunscreen, and something on your feet!" You're done.

"So, Sara, you can make your bed, sweep under your bed, or put your dirty laundry in your laundry bag. Which task do you want to do first?" You're done.

"Put the paper right on top of the oil cloth, and then tape it down, using the masking tape and put your name on the paper in the lower right corner." You're finished until they complete those three instructions. In fact, if the instructions are more complicated, like the ones in this particular example, you may even be better off giving them out one-by-one.

Key point #23: Repeat back to me.

Another technique to use with younger children or children who have ADD (attention deficit disorder) or ADHD (attention deficit hyperactive disorder) is to have the campers repeat back to you what you just talked about doing. For example, the three things you ask them to bring to the pool—"a towel, sunscreen, and something on your feet." Asking a camper to repeat directions you have just given out forces them to actually locate that knowledge in their mind, which requires an active posture, not just a passive one. It also helps ensure that the listener will actually commit what was just said to longer-term memory. For example, "So, James, what is it you need to bring to the pool?" "So, Sarah, what is it you're taking with you to the waterfront?"

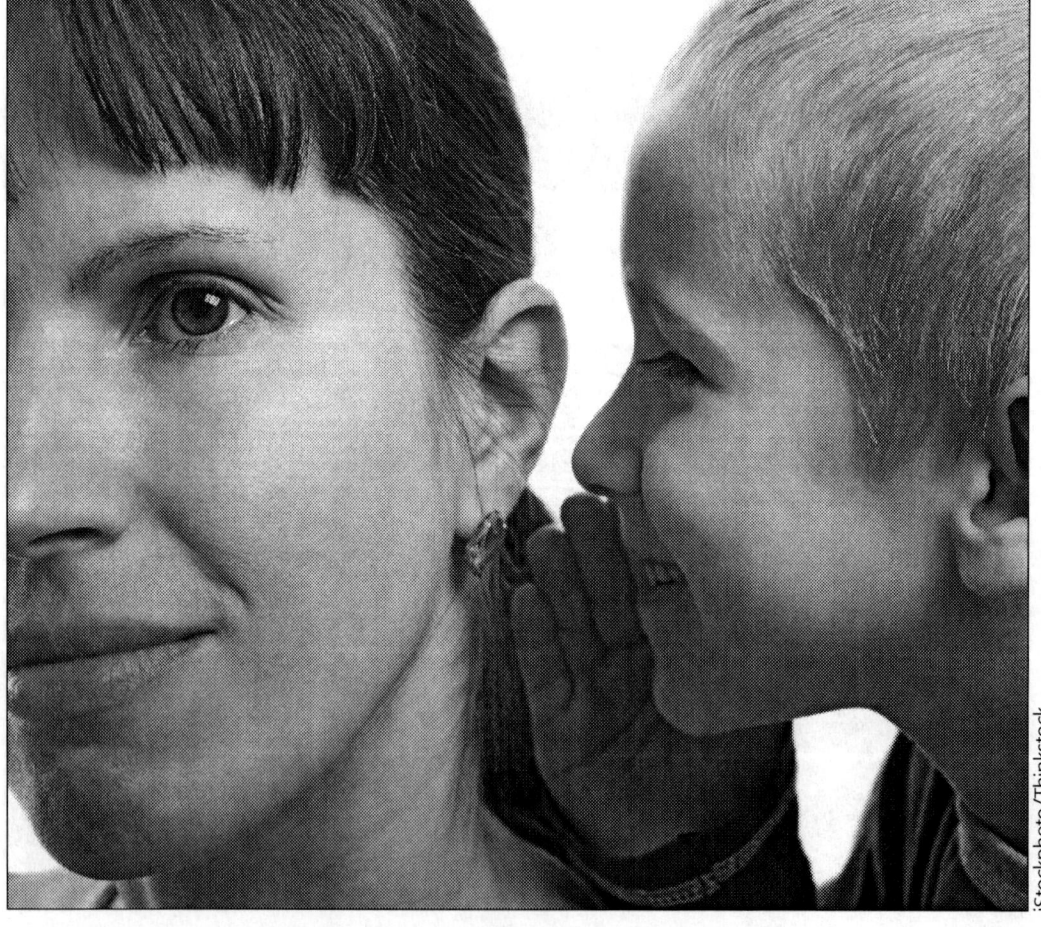

iStockphoto/Thinkstock

Key point #24: Tag teaming campers.

In reality, some of your campers will require more attention than others. Furthermore, some campers are less impulsive, more consistent, less moody, or more organized than others. For example, a child who has ADD may need you to break things down into shorter directions, give them three things to do at a time, have them repeat back to you what you just said, and praise them more frequently. Working with this camper will likely be more taxing than interacting with a camper needing half that amount of time and energy, which is why I suggest you and your co-counselor take turns or tag team certain campers. In other words, one counselor takes them under their wing during cleanup, while the other one of you works with them at bedtime.

Tag teaming campers not only helps you and your co-counselor(s) feel more like the workload is being more evenly distributed, it also helps that camper become familiar with all of their counselors, not just one. It is always better to have campers be able to work and respond positively to as many counselors as possible since you aren't always going to be around the next time that camper needs help.

iStockphoto/Thinkstock

Key point #25: Less is more (brevity revisited).

One of the four most common mistakes adults make with children is we talk too much. As was previously pointed out in the discussion about brevity, the more we continue talking about something, the harder we make it for a child to absorb our point or lesson. They can't digest what we've said if we are forcing them to keep listening.

This factor is such a critical feature of communication with children that it needs its own section. As was previously noted, children today are used to making decisions from the very short bits of information they get from a variety of sources, such as e-mail, text, i-Chat®, BBM, or IM. Their brains are trained to pick up essential messages, based on very concise exchanges of information. Being brief requires work on our part as the speaker. Being brief forces us to think about exactly what our essential message is and how to say it succinctly enough that kids can easily absorb it. It is an art form all its own. People who are more successful with children know when to speak up, know how to keep it short and sweet, and know when to stop talking. They're also great at texting. Lol!

iStockphoto/Thinkstock

Key point #26: We get too emotional.

Another common mistake adults make with children is that they get too emotional. We get too angry, too worried, too disappointed, and maybe even too excited. I'm not saying that it isn't normal to have feelings like these. It's just not always helpful to express strong emotion when we are disciplining kids or getting them to listen to us. If we are too emotional, our message may get lost, because kids are too busy reacting to the emotion rather than the ideas we are expressing. As I once said to a father: "What you have to say to your son is too important for it to get lost in your temper. If you get too angry, there is a danger that he will react so strongly to how upset you are that he won't hear a word you're saying. What's the gain in that?"

If you remember my advice about dropping the rope (point 13), you will recall that the very first part of that formula is staying calm. It's not that you can't say you're angry, disappointed, upset, or whatever you are experiencing. Doing so makes you real. You just want to make sure that the emotion you convey is balanced and doesn't dilute the message you want to impart. When I do a role-play in front of counselors demonstrating an intervention with a camper, one of the things I constantly hear when we debrief is how calm my voice seems. I know it is easier for me to role-play a scene and be calm than it is to be in the middle of a group of 8 to 15 campers on a busy, hot summer day. That said, the more you can keep a cool head and be even-handed in your interactions with campers, the more they will listen to you. Keeping your cool will make you more effective.

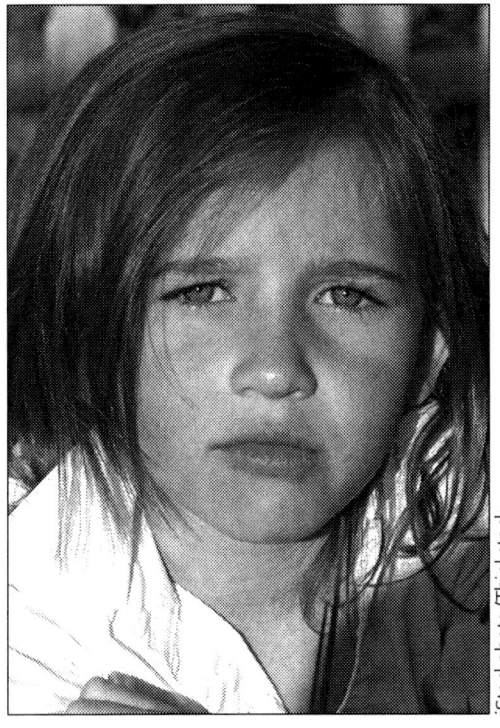

iStockphoto/Thinkstock

Key point #27: Redirecting behavior

Redirecting behavior basically means changing the focus of a child from one activity to another. More often than not, the activity we move the child away from is one that is potentially harmful or simply inappropriate. The idea is to channel the energy and attention of the child and simply direct it into an activity that is safer, more appropriate, or more beneficial. For example, let's say you walk into a cabin and discover a child jumping up and down on the top of a bunk bed. You immediately realize that this situation is somewhat precarious. So, instead of telling the child to stop, you invite them to join you in a game of Nerf® basketball, jacks, or something similar. Instead of interrupting the child's energy, you "redirect" that energy into a safer activity. Obviously, the more you deliver your invitation with excitement and energy of your own, the more likely the child will comply.

Redirecting is a strategy used by parents and childcare workers all the time. A baby sitting in a high chair throwing food can easily be distracted from that pastime simply by jangling a set of keys in front of them. A three-year-old trying to take a toy from another child who is already playing with it can often be distracted away from their thievery by an adult who will play with them. Similarly, at camp, redirecting a child's behavior can help keep the positive energy flowing, while avoiding accidents or mishaps.

Jupiterimages

Key point #28: Pivoting—from "best friend" to "authority"

Times will exist when you will be talking or playing with some of your campers when you realize that you need to switch gears and get them to get ready for the next activity period. Or maybe you've been hanging out with them in the cabin at night, and you realize you need to have them get ready for bed. You find yourself needing to go from being a sort of "best friend" to being the counselor who needs to make things happen.

This factor is a critical pivoting point—one that requires a bit of deft handling on your part if you don't want to alienate your campers. Because the campers are experiencing you one way, as a friend or a buddy, when you change roles or suddenly "pivot," it may feel abrupt and startling to them. The best way to handle the change in your role is to do the following:

- First, acknowledge the good time you just had with your campers.
- Then, announce that you are about to change your role from friend to authority.
- Then, finally, begin giving directions to your campers.

All-in-all, it might sound something like the following:

"Hey, guys, this was really fun. I like talking with you guys. You've all got great ideas about these things. I also just realized that rest hour is about to end, so we've got to get ready to go to our afternoon activities. I'm sorry we have to end this now, but I'm going to have to get up and get the other guys ready, too. But let's make sure we get to talk like this again sometime."

Background: What I realized a couple of years ago is that many children these days have a close personal relationship with their parents and are often used to talking with their parents like friends. Paradoxically, there are also times when their parents have their heads buried in their PDAs (Blackberries® or i-Phones®) so that they don't seem truly present. As a result, children today are especially sensitive to moments when an adult gives them attention and when that same adult withdraws their attention. The transitions you are constantly being asked to make at camp, like from rest hour to afternoon activities, or from hanging out to going to bed, will go so much more smoothly if you take the time to make this transitional acknowledgment part of your skill set.

Key point #29: Sarcasm

Several years ago, I was at a boys' resident camp, waiting near the flagpole for the morning assembly to start. It was 7:30 in the morning. The boys had just been woken up for the day and were coming down to the basketball court where the morning assembly took place. Just before the meeting was about to begin, one of the counselors standing near me looked back up the hill leading down to the assembly area and noticed that more than a few of his campers had not yet arrived. He yelled back up the hill something like, "Hey, guys! My old grandmother can run faster than you! What's the matter, girls? Didn't get your morning make-up on in time?"

The counselor's voice was dripping in sarcasm and his comments were loud enough for everyone to hear. Some of the boys who were already seated in their groups chuckled at the remarks, while the 10-year-olds running down the hill just took it in stride. The assembly moved on, and no one seemed worse for the wear.

Check back with that same 10-year-old cabin a day or two later, and see how those same boys are being sarcastic to one another. They will grate on each other and insult each other all in the name of "being funny." Their own sarcastic behavior demonstrates two things: first, children will mimic everything they see (refer to the next point, "mirroring"); and second, sarcasm has no place in camp.

Brain researchers tell us that the human brain does not "get" sarcasm until about age 14, because sarcasm in its best form combines two paradoxical ingredients: aggression and affection. Sarcasm is a kind of humor that a person might use only with a good friend, an individual who is likely to "get" not just the barb, but the affection in which it is wrapped. For a brain that is not yet 14 years old, an "affectionate barb" is a contradiction in terms. To appreciate the affection that accompanies the jab, our brains have to be mature enough to put together two apparently disparate elements—aggression and affection.

This point does not mean that children under the age of 14 don't use sarcasm—they certainly do. But, they use sarcasm as a weapon, not as a way of poking fun at a friend with some warmth to it. If you have ever been in a cabin with a group of kids who characteristically use sarcasm with one another, you know just how oppressive it can be.

Most counselors I have observed, and especially male counselors, use a lot of sarcasm with campers. It is an insidious and infectious habit—one that is hard to catch yourself doing and one that is hard to stop. However, if you truly want to create a less hostile environment among your campers, you will not only curb your own use of sarcasm, you will also limit the use of sarcasm by your campers.

Key point #30: Mirroring

In the last few years, a lot of exciting brain research has been undertaken throughout the world. One of the more interesting discoveries is what neuro-scientists call "mirror neurons," cells in the brain whose sole purpose is to mimic everything they experience. (*Brain Rules,* John Medina, Pear Press, Seattle, pp. 269-270). When a child sees another person do something, they often mimic what they have seen. Some people call this the "monkey see, money do" phenomenon. At camp, the five-year-old boys who march stridently behind their charismatic counselor are all soon wearing their baseball caps just like he is. The nine-year-old girls in lower camp sneak peeks at the camp dance and later practice the same moves in their cabin at bedtime they saw the older girls exhibit while dancing in the lodge just minutes earlier.

It turns out that as many as 50 percent of the 100 billion neurons in our brains are dedicated to one thing: mimicking everything they experience. (*A User's Guide to the Brain,* John J. Ratey, MD, Random House, pp. 9 and 267). As a counselor, the good news is that everything you do and say, especially things you may not even realize you are doing and saying, your campers will repeat. The bad news is that everything you do and say will also be repeated by your campers. This is what it means to be a "role model"—someone after whom the campers will shape their own behavior. As social creatures, we learn from one another, both the good habits and the bad ones. Not surprisingly, most parents and camp directors are hoping that more of your good habits "rub off" on the campers than your bad ones. The point is that, unlike most any job you have had to date, being a camp counselor requires that you actually pay attention to your own behavior, and not just the behavior of the kids.

Hemera/Thinkstock

Key point #31: Walk and talk, and one-on-one time.

One of the more effective ways of "getting through" to a camper is having what I call a "walk and talk." When you are trying to establish a stronger or more influential connection between yourself and a particular camper, doing something with them while you are talking can be helpful. Obviously, if what you are doing is too absorbing, like going down a zip line, not much talking is going to take place. One activity with an easy kind of rhythm that provides just enough action without distracting from the conversation is walking. Since you naturally walk from activity to activity throughout the camp day, it is easy to utilize it as a way of making a better connection with a particular camper or a small group of campers.

A "walk and talk" can happen naturally if you set it up carefully. One way to do this is to arrange to have your co-counselor take the other kids ahead, while you walk alone and slightly behind the rest of the group. You may want to take the camper aside and ask them to "help you out" with something at the end of the activity. Or, you may simply be direct about it and invite them to walk with you over to the next activity. Doing so allows the other campers to move ahead with their co-counselor, leaving you to walk one-on-one with the camper with whom you want to connect.

A more deliberate approach would be to set up a "walk and talk" routinely with each of your campers, taking a little personal time with each camper as a way of getting to know them better. Having some undivided, one-on-one time with each camper will enhance your connection with them, which in turn may allow you to influence their behavior more positively as a result.

Boys, in particular, seem to be able to engage in conversation more casually when they are somewhat active. Besides taking a walk with a boy, I've played catch, participated in a one-on-one card game, or gone down to a lake or pond and skipped stones, while engaging them in conversation. This kind of low level of activity has an almost calming effect on many boys.

One word of caution: when you take any camper for a walk, for your own protection, you will want to stay within the guidelines of appropriate contact with children. You should make sure you are never completely out of eyesight of other adults when you are one-on-one with a camper. You can be several yards or half a field away, be visible to others, and still have enough privacy to have a meaningful personal conversation with a camper.

Key point #32: Keep them busy!

As every teacher, childcare specialist, or experienced counselor will tell you, the more you keep your campers energetically involved in activities, the less homesickness you will have, the fewer discipline problems you will have, and the more fun everyone will have. Two particular times a wise counselor plans for at camp are rest hour and early morning.

Especially later in the session, campers will often be tired enough at rest hour that they may actually nap. However, most campers will need quiet time activities to keep them out of trouble (or to help prevent them from getting homesick in the earlier days of a session). Having some playing cards, checkers, chess, jacks, drawing materials, or other quiet-time activities on hand will provide you with a little more peace during rest hour.

The early morning hours, before the rest of your cabin is awake, can be particularly difficult for younger or homesick campers who are early risers. To help keep them occupied, and again, to help keep them from wandering off or waking other campers up, having some quiet-time activities on hand and set out near their bed is good planning. For example, you can use drawing materials, or have Sudoku or other puzzles, letter-writing supplies, or even materials for making a camp bracelet or arm band on hand. Talk with a camper who seems to get homesick in the early morning before the rush of activities takes over and see what ideas the two of you can come up with. As long as it is something that they can do quietly and doesn't require anything too special, if it will help take their mind off their homesickness it is worth giving a try.

One idea I have used with campers who are especially homesick is to have them keep a kind of drawing "diary," in which they draw a picture in a tablet of drawing paper of each day at camp. When they wake up n the morning, they draw a picture of the preceding day. They can draw the thing they did that day they liked the most and add whatever details they want, like a new friend they made or something special they may have had at a meal.

Another idea is to have them make a paper bracelet. Each new paper loop is decorated and represents a single day at camp. The loops can be as simple or elaborate as the camper wants to make them. If this activity is something they can do if they wake up earlier than everyone else, just make sure the materials they need are at their bedside the night before.

Key point #33: Ask for help.

By now, it should be clear that working successfully with children means collecting ideas and strategies over time. Anyone I know whose work with campers I admire has acquired ideas from many people over time, myself included. As I have pointed out before, some counselors are reluctant to ask for help with a particular camper or a group of campers for one of several possible reasons, including the following:

- They are afraid that they might appear like they don't know what they are doing.
- They are afraid that they may have made some mistakes with a camper that might come to light during a conversation with a unit director or head counselor.
- They feel, unreasonably, that asking for help is a sign of weakness.

Asking for help is actually smart. Knowing when you need another perspective or an idea about how to do something with a camper with whom you haven't been able to achieve your specific goals simply means you are giving yourself and the camper a better chance of succeeding. An environment that is so competitive that it punishes counselors for admitting what they do not know and for availing themselves of help is not a healthy place for either campers or staff.

7

More Advanced Communication Skills and Strategies With Campers

Mykola Velychko

Many of the points covered in Chapter 6 are like building blocks in that you will use them when you engage in more complex strategies like those addressed here in chapter 7. Invariably, a time will come when a camper will be even more resistant to your authority as a counselor or will have difficulties with other campers that will require additional strategies. The techniques in this chapter have been developed over time and have been tried by many counselors. If you have never used one of these practices before it would be best to read it over and discuss it both with a co-counselor and a supervisor, like a unit director, division leader, head counselor, or director. The more you can "picture" yourself using one of these skills, the more likely it will go well and be successful.

Key point #34: The "respect" conversation

The interventions presented in the previous chapter are what I call the *first line of defense.* They are the basic skills that every counselor should have and use as much as humanly possible. On the other hand, a time will always come when you will have "dropped the rope," taken a child aside, and done just about everything else you can possibly think of without getting any appreciable improvement in the child's behavior. At that point, you need the "respect conversation."

You start by taking the camper aside and making a simple statement about the problem. Let's say it is about participating in clean-up. The conversation might go as follows: "Jason, we've talked before about making your bed and cleaning up in the cabin, just like all the other guys. So, what I want to know is, if I ask you in a respectful way to clean up, are you telling me you're going to refuse me? Is that what you're telling me?"

To be able to make the statement above in a way that actually carries maximum impact, you need to attend to the following conditions:

- You will have to make every reasonable effort to have engaged Jason in cleaning up *before* resorting to this method.
- You will have to discuss the consequences *beforehand* with your supervisor.
- You will have to take Jason aside, somewhere away from the other campers, to have this conversation.
- You will need to speak with Jason in a calm manner—*no matter how agitated he might get.*
- All of your interactions with Jason up to this point will need to have been executed by you in a respectful manner. If you have raised your voice, sworn at him, or threatened him, it will only *weaken* your position, which Jason will most likely use against you.
- You will need to follow the recommended script—the actual wording—as closely as possible. It is worded in such a way so as to place the camper at a critical point of choosing.

Once you have spoken, allow what you have said to sink in. You need to remain calm and quietly in control. What you are essentially doing is bringing to Jason's attention the fact that the issue between you and he is no longer about cleaning up, but about *him not recognizing your authority as the counselor.* It is one thing for a camper to occasionally resist a staff member's directions. At some point, however, if the camper consistently refuses to go along with your reasonable camp-sanctioned requests ("everybody knows cleanup is part of camp"), you have a problem of a different order.

At this point most campers will back down. *If they do, you are not finished.* You then ask the camper the following: "So, are you telling me I can count on you to make your bed and to clean up?" It is important that you calmly ask the camper to tell you just what it is you can count on them for. "So, what is it you're going to do when we go back into the cabin? I just want to make sure I've got it right." Once you go back into the cabin,

---

give the camper some space and a moment to save face. Provide the camper with the opportunity to do what they promised to do. *If you hover over them at this point,* it will be perceived by the camper as a provocation on your part. Everyone needs to save face. Once you "win" the argument, let the temperature come down a bit.

If the camper can tell you specifically what they are going to do, and then *follows through,* you have made your point. If they do not follow through, then you must wait until the end of the cleanup period (or whatever period it is) and take the camper aside and say, "We obviously have a problem, since you are not willing to do what I ask you, even though it is what every other camper does and even though I have asked you in a really respectful way. So, I will set up a conversation with the head counselor and we'll all sit down and work it out." If the camper presses you about when that will be, you should simply and calmly say that you will get back to them. At that point, both of you go about your business.

If, when you first speak to the camper, they do not back down but confirm that they are not going to comply with your directive, then you say, "So, then you and I have a problem, and I'll have to make arrangements for us to talk with the division leader (or similar in your camp) so we can work this out."

You should note that you are saying, "we" have a problem, not the camper has the problem. While it may be that you do not have this challenge with any other camper, the problem is *between* the two of you. It is your willingness to remain calm and to look the camper in the eye and not shrink away from the conflict that carries impact. As I mentioned previously, you should tell the camper that you will get back to them and then go about your business.

Since you will have spoken with your supervisor about the situation *before* invoking the respect conversation, your supervisor will know what is going on when you report back to them. At some point, as soon as it can be arranged, you and the camper will meet with the supervisor. The conversation will then resume, except this time the head counselor or division leader will take the lead. If your supervisor is smart, they will first take a little time to "join" with the camper in a bit of small talk, like how long the camper has been coming to camp, what they like best about camp, or anything else that is relatively safe and non-threatening. At some point, it would be beneficial if your supervisor could share with the camper some positive qualities the camper may have *that you have told your supervisor about.* Going back to my discussion of charity, clarity, brevity, and levity, this tact would be *charitable* in a way that may help the camper be more receptive and less defensive. The point of being charitable even when the camper has been disrespectful or resistant to your authority is to send the message that you are not meeting to humiliate him or her, but to help him or her be the best camper they can be.

The conversation, again led by the supervisor, would go as follows: "So, Jason, Mike, your counselor, also tells me that you refuse to make your bed and clean up like the rest of your cabin mates. He tells me that even when he asks you in a really respectful way to clean up, you refuse him. Is that right?"

What is important in the ensuing conversation is that the feelings the camper may express—his anger about having to clean up at all, how stupid making a bed is, how dumb this camp is—should be acknowledged and separated from what you expect. In other words, it is *fine* that the camper feels whatever he feels. His feelings are *his* business. However, what the camper needs to commit to is *listening to his counselor.* Once an agreement is made, the supervisor must make a point of telling the camper that he will be checking in with the two of you in a day or so to see how things are going.

During the conversation, the camper may reveal something else that may require attention. For example, it may come out that he is homesick, or that his parents are getting a divorce, or that he never sees his father at home, or that he never wanted to come to camp in the first place. Each of these issues can be addressed as they come up and may require your supervisor to call the camper's parents, a factor that is for your supervisor to sort out.

In the event the camper is as defiant with the supervisor as he or she is with you, your supervisor would take over and have a meeting with the director and the camper, which would eventually include a phone call home.

iStockphoto/Thinkstock

Key point #35: "Everybody knows..."

One of the most important assets you can develop for working with children is a set of useful phrases that will help you establish trust, make a point, or elicit a response from a child. One such phrase is "everybody knows." It has two distinct uses with two different meanings.

The first use of the phrase is an attempt to depersonalize a conflict a camper might have with you, the counselor. For example, in the preceding situation where the camper is resistant to making their bed, you might say, "Everybody knows that cleanup is just a regular part of camp. We do it every day." Using the phrase this way allows you to normalize most any aspect of camp that a child might be resisting. For example, "Everybody knows that when you come to camp, you go to activities." Another might be, "Everybody knows that campers aren't allowed to go off into the woods or down to the waterfront without a counselor." In this way, you are not only defusing the conflict between you and a resistant camper, but you are also attempting to invoke common knowledge. Cleaning up, going to activities, staying with the group, turning the lights out, taking a shower, and helping out are all examples of the normal, everyday aspects of camp, and *everybody knows that*.

A second way exists to use the phrase that is more delicate and requires more skill and a careful delivery. Times will exist when a child's behavior is so unusual or so striking that it is hard not to conclude that something is going on that has nothing to do with the present situation. For example, in the preceding situation, where the camper is resistant to cleaning up, you might wonder why a child would go to such extreme lengths simply to get out of making a bed. If, at some point, I thought there might be some other issue bothering a child that was being played out or expressed through their resistance to cleaning up, I might say something like the following:

"It's pretty clear, Jason, that cleanup brings up some pretty strong feelings in you. There aren't too many kids who go to such lengths, just to get out of making a bed. Everybody knows when a kid has such strong feelings about something as ordinary as making a bed, something's not right. Now, I might be wrong, but it seems to me that something is making you have some pretty strong feelings, and somehow I don't think making a bed is it."

The idea is to let a child know that strong feelings don't come from mundane things. It is a line best used after a single specific episode where a child's strong feelings are apparent. For example, if I had a camper who just had an out-of-proportion temper flare-up, I might use the phrase. "Everybody knows that when a kid gets as upset as you just did a little while ago, something's not right. That was like a 50 dollar reaction to a five-dollar crime, which makes me wonder where the other 45 bucks is coming from." Again, if you can't deliver the line without putting the child on the defensive, then don't use it this way. If you can signal a child that you are trying to help them, the phrase just may open up a conversation that will lead to a better understanding of the situation. The line cannot be used for children whose behavior is more chronic or has organic roots, such as hyperactivity, eating disorders, or cutting.

Key point #36: Secret signal

A secret signal is something you use with a camper when you want to discretely prompt them discretely about their behavior. For example, if a camper has a temper problem, and you begin to see that they are beginning to lose it, you might invoke the secret signal. The signal might be a tap on the shoulder or a certain phrase you agree on, like, "Hey, has anybody heard the baseball scores from last night?"

A secret signal can also be set up as a way of enabling a camper to let you know about something that might be embarrassing to them were they to say it out loud. For example, if a child has a bedwetting problem, having a secret signal (like discreetly putting their water bottle upside down on the top shelf of the cubby) allows them to alert you to any problem, without the other kids knowing.

The point of employing the secret signal is to bring a certain behavior to a child's awareness so that they can exercise greater self-restraint. The point of a camper using it with you is to signal you that they may need help or may need to go to a prearranged area or into a prearranged action plan. For example, in the case of a kid who is beginning to lose their temper, they may "signal" you that they are taking a self-imposed "timeout" as an attempt not to lose their temper and get into trouble. (See the next point on "cooling off spots"). On the other hand, you may have a child who needs to use the bathroom and signals you discreetly that that is where they are going. Secret signals can be used in many arrangements with campers when you want a communication to be more private.

iStockphoto/Thinkstock

Key point #37: Cooling-off spot

The cooling-off spot is something I use with kids who have difficulty controlling their tempers. You arrange the spot with the camper as part of a plan to help them reduce their temper outbursts. If going to a prearranged area to cool of helps them regain their composure, then it may be a great investment in that child's peace of mind as well as the peace of mind of their cabin mates.

The cooling-off spot should be near the cabin in which the camper lives or the activity area the child frequents. It can be a picnic table, a tree, a bench, a bush, the end of a porch, or just a grassy area that is easy for the child to get to. It should be a place that is within eyesight of other counselors, some of whom may need to be told about the secret spot so they don't pepper the camper with questions about why they are there. If another camper wants to know where the kid is going, I just say he's getting a breather.

Some camp professionals have asked me if permitting a camper to go to a cooling-off spot to calm down and regain their composure creates resentment on the part of other campers. They wonder whether the child will use it simply to get out of things, like cleanup. This inquiry is a legitimate question, though in my experience, most of the time, the other campers are quietly relieved that the kid with the temper is cooling off. As for the notion that a child might use it to avoid work or responsibilities, if that seems to be happening, it can always be discussed. A counselor can always give the camper a moment or two, and then head over to the spot and check in with the camper, thus paving the way for the camper's return.

Hemera/Thinkstock

Key point #38: "I don't want the other kids to get the wrong idea about you…!"

This statement is another useful phrase that you can use when talking with a camper who may have a behavior problem. When I am having a more intensive one-on-one talk with a camper, and I get to the point in the conversation where I need to be clear about an aspect of their behavior that is inappropriate, I try to employ language that may make it easier for the child to tolerate what I am saying.

An example might be if a camper had a habit of saying rude things to other campers when they got upset. What I might say would be something like, "I understand why you say things like that. You get frustrated and upset and you lash out. You and I both know you're just hurt and angry, but I'm concerned the other kids might get the wrong idea about you. They might start thinking that you're a rude person! That would not only be terrible, it's not true!"

Obviously, this reasoning is a line that you employ only after the child has calmed down and can be engaged in a more reflective way. It helps, too, if you take some time to be *charitable* with the camper by acknowledging a few of their strengths or laudable accomplishments at camp. If you try talking with a child too soon after they have been upset, their adrenalin levels will simply be too high, and they will be reactive to most anything you say.

If I make this point to a camper who then responds by saying that they don't care what the other kids think, I calmly and clearly say, "Well, I care. I know you're a good kid. Your feelings just sometimes get the best of you!" After all, in most cases with kids, this statement is true.

The beauty of this line is that you can use it to point out behavior that would normally elicit a defensive reaction from a child. It allows you to point out most any behavior, because it is not *you, the counselor, who thinks this about the child;* it is your *concern* that the *other kids* might think this about the child. You are just trying to save them from a colossal case of misunderstanding. Key point #42, discussed later in this chapter, presents an idea of how this line might be used in a more developed conversation with a camper.

Key point #39: "You and I both know … "

I use this line when I am talking with a child, and I want to engage their healthier, reflective, more reasonable side. "You and I both know you can do this if you put your mind to it."

As you can see by this example, it is only used in a positive way to reinforce or draw out a coping skill or positive quality in a child. "You and I both know you can be a really great friend. So, sometimes you get a little upset. Who doesn't! You and I both know that you have more good days than bad."

iStockphoto/Thinkstock

Key point #40: "Play-date" at camp

"Play-date at camp" is a detailed method for helping shy or socially awkward campers make new friends. You use it when a camper in your group is struggling to fit in or be part of the group and doesn't seem to be having much success.

Before I describe how it works. I want to point out that not all children are comfortable in group situations. Some youngsters make friends more easily in smaller groups or in one-on-one settings. As such, they feel overwhelmed or shy in a larger group. Play-date at camp is designed to help these campers.

The initial phase of the plan is to have a private talk with the camper who is struggling to fit in or make friends. After acknowledging their feelings, ask them if they could spend time with any one or two campers out of the whole group, whom would they choose? You have to be careful here because some children will choose the most popular camper. While this is understandable, it may not be the most realistic move. Help the camper choose one or two campers from their group with whom you think they have a more realistic chance of becoming friends with.

The next step is to find a time when you can take the two or three campers on the "play-date." The activity itself should be something you can easily arrange (talk with your supervisor about ideas). It should be something fun, like baking cookies, roasting marshmallows at a campfire site (boys in particular love making fires), or going swimming together (as long as you can be in a group by yourselves away from other groups). If your campers are younger, and you have animals on camp, going to visit and feed the animals together can also be fun.

Setting up and executing the play-date is usually pretty easy to do. What is more challenging is managing the expectations of the shy or awkward camper. It is critical that you take time to explain to the camper that while you are together at the activity, you will probably all have a great time. You also need to prepare the camper for the liklihood that the one or two kids they go on the play-date with will go right back to their other cabin friends once they return from their time together. Explain that it takes time to make a new friend and that the play-date is designed to help them get started. It is not going to make them instant friends. Adding this bit of caution will help the camper be less deflated when they return and the other two campers do exactly what you said they would do—join back up with their other friends.

Another complication of the play-date is when other campers find out about it. You can just hear their complaint! "Hey! How come we don't get to do that?" My answer is simple: "Maybe sometime you can!" What I mean is that it makes sense to schedule a few play-dates—maybe three a week if you can manage it—and vary the kids whom you ask to come along. Doing so would not only include other campers, it would also expose the shy camper to more kids in smaller groups.

Once you start having play-dates, you will also need to speak with your co-counselor about how to balance the time you spend on them with your other responsibilities. After all, being with two to three campers for an entire period takes you away from other campers. You will need to work out the scheduling details with your supervisor in such a way that your co-counselor doesn't get saddled with all of the other campers all of the time.

One final point can be shared about play-dates. Since the underlying objective of the plan is to help shy or socially awkward campers get a foothold on some friendships, another great thing to do as an adjunct to that effort is to start a game of cards with one or two campers during rest hour and invite the shy camper to join you. This step will help reinforce the friendships they may have started to make on the play-date. If you are thoughtful, you can probably find a number of ways to initiate a small-group activity and invite that camper to join you.

iStockphoto/Thinkstock

Key point #41: Special job/counselor's helper

One great way to build rapport with a camper is to have them help you do some legitimate job at camp. The most commonly used "special job" is going to get the mail from the office. Another might be going with you to get snacks for the other campers.

With younger children at day camp, having them hold your clipboard is a good way to help a child who otherwise wanders to stay with the group. Another possible "job" at day camp is to have a child lead the line of campers from one activity area to the next. When the other campers begin to complain that the same child has been getting that privilege again and again, give that child the "job" of helping you choose which camper gets to lead the group next.

Activity areas can also encompass various special jobs. For example, going with you to check in on the horses is one. Keeping the scores during a sports match is another. Going with you to get the equipment for a sports match is yet another.

The point of special jobs is to "redirect" a camper's energy or attention or to create a stringer bond with them—one that allows you to influence their behavior in a more positive direction.

Jupiterimages

Key point #42: "Hot head"—helping boys with their anger

Ever encounter a boy who has a terrible temper? Sometimes they throw things, swear, threaten others, or run away. Once they have cooled down, they often promise never to do it again, only to lose their temper later. "Hot head" is designed to help you help these children. The primary objective of the technique is to help a child gain control over their temper or angry feelings so they can have more success at camp (as well as everywhere else).

To initially employ "hot head," a meeting should be set up with the child, one of the child's counselors (the one who is closest to him) and the counselor's supervisor (e.g., the boys' head counselor or someone similar). The supervisor and counselor will review the purpose and tactics of the meeting before getting the camper. The meeting will be run by the supervisor and will unfold as follows:

- **Part One**—Joining: Engage in some non-threatening small talk about camp, what the camper likes most about camp, how long they have been coming to camp, and so on. The supervisor will ask the counselor for some examples of how this boy has been helpful or for some other positive things the counselor can say about the boy that are real and therefore credible. This phase is the *charitable* portion of the talk that will set you up for the *clarity* portion, which comes next.

- **Part Two**—Name the behavior: Without shaming the child, state specific examples of his behavior that have been observed by the counselor. Be clear and give one or two specific examples, such as, "Like yesterday, when you were down at tennis, and the referee called one of your balls out of bounds, and you got really angry and stormed off the court." The underlying premise behind providing one or two specific examples is to be clear about the boy's behavior, not to shame him.

- **Part Three**—Making an intervention. I start with this line: "I don't think you like it when you lose your temper. And I'll tell you why I think that. First, it's embarrassing for you. Then, you get into trouble and have to talk to people like me, and we know that's a drag. If that weren't bad enough, then the other kids start to tease you or egg you on. As such, if you lose your temper, they don't get into trouble for it, you do! And *that* stinks."

Then go on to clarify that the reason the boy's counselor brought him to the supervisor is because he wants to help him with his temper. "It's like you've got this big *thing* on your back called 'your temper' and it just gets the best of you from time to time. Besides, I don't want the other kids to get the wrong idea about you. They might start to think you're a hot head or something. We know you're a good kid, but if you keep losing your temper, they might just think you're a bad kid."

Executing "hot head" involves establishing a safe "cooling-off place," where the camper has permission to go that is within eyesight of the cabin or activity area, where he can calm himself down and avoid losing his temper. This step will give him a way to regain control and will help him avoid getting into trouble or hurting others. All of his counselors should know about this "safe place," which is also known as the "time-out spot." I make it clear that going there is not a punishment. To go to the "safe place" is smart because it helps that camper stay out of trouble. Have the child develop a secret sign with their counselor as a way of letting them know that they are taking off for the "spot." The next step is to pull out a stress or Koosh® ball and place it in the camper's hand. This action initiates the second phase of the "hot head" plan. This phase incorporates the following three elements: the procedure, the practice, and the promise:

The procedure: this segment requires you to utilize this script: "This is your temper (looking at the ball in the camper's hand)." You should then wait a second or two and swipe the ball out of the camper's hand, and then state, "Oh, my goodness! You just lost your temper! No wonder you have so much trouble! You can't hold onto your temper! You want to try that again?"

Then, replace the ball in the camper's hand and tell them to "hold on this time!" There are ground rules to the activity, for example, like the boy can't stand up, he can only use one hand, and he must let you get an equal grip on the ball. Have the counselor who is watching say, "Go!" While the boy is trying to hold on to that ball, you will be trying to wrest it free, all the while encouraging him to, "Hold on to your temper!" It is important to really cheer the camper on! "That's right! Hold on to your temper! You've got it! Hold on to it! You're doing great!" These comments are all said *while you are trying your hardest to get the ball out of his hand.*

The practice: "Now, I want you to have this same contest twice a day with your counselor." In fact, have the counselor and the camper try it again right there.

The promise: Make a specific time to check back with the camper and the counselor to see whether the boy has been using his "time-out spots" and whether he and his counselor have been "practicing" the temper exercise with the ball.

To be sure, while the little wrestling exercise with the tennis ball is a gimmick, it does help make the boy feel that his counselor is trying to help him. It also serves as a fun reminder that he is working on controlling his temper.

8

Counselor Group Skills:
In the Cabin, Tent, or Group

Stockbyte

A lot of the skills that counselors spend time learning are those that are useful in one-on-one situations with campers. Ironically, most of the time that you will spend with your campers will be in groups. Campers live in groups, go to and participate in activities in groups, eat in groups, play sports on teams or groups, travel to other camps in groups, and go to campfires or special events in groups. This chapter addresses exclusively group skills, from the most elementary to the more advanced. The best camp counselors are those individuals who can be as effective with campers in groups as they can one-on-one.

When I talk with counselors about so-called bunk or cabin meetings, the most often-cited reason for having to meet with campers is to "talk out problems in the group." For several reasons, it would be unfortunate if most of your meetings with campers were spent "talking out problems" or discussing the troubles in the group. First, if the only time you meet with campers is when there is trouble, campers will soon begin to associate meetings with being in trouble and will come to resist and resent meetings. In addition, so many useful reasons exist for having meetings, especially if they are short and well thought out, that it is a shame to reserve them only for talking out problems.

Being able to have meetings that are fun or useful depends in large part on your mastery of group-meeting skills and etiquette. The 22 points covered in this chapter are designed to help you be the best you can be in running crisp, well-focused meetings that campers will appreciate.

Hemera/Thinkstock

Key point #43: Meeting etiquette

Most counselors have never really run a meeting before they come to camp, let alone a meeting with children. They simply jump in and hope for the best. A little forethought and awareness of what I call "meeting etiquette," or protocols and practices that enable meetings to move along smoothly, is the best place to start. Proper meeting etiquette includes the following:

- *Plan your meetings ahead of time.* No one likes to go to a meeting that is a waste of time or poorly planned. Campers are no exception.
- *Script the meeting with your co-counselor.* Doing so might take just a couple of minutes, but the investment of time is worth the confusion you will avoid. Know ahead of time who is starting the meeting, what the main points are, and how long the meeting will last. Some of the best meetings are relatively brief ones, where something specific gets done—or resolved. And if they're short and productive, campers may actually look forward to them.
- *Be clear about what the objective of the meeting is, announce it to the campers right at the start, and then stick to it.* One of the things that people resent about meetings is when they come expecting one agenda, only to discover another one entirely.
- *Sit in a circle,* when possible, with as few obstacles as possible. When people sit in a circle everyone can see everyone else. There is no beginning or end. Circles are the best format for meetings.
- *Vary the agenda for your meetings.* You can have a meeting to give out jobs on the cleanup "job wheel," plan a skit for talent night, praise your campers for their great efforts at cleanup, or talk about the white water rafting trip you are all taking tomorrow. As long as you practice the four principles that were outlined in Chapter 4—you are upbeat, clear, light-hearted (when appropriate) and brief, the meetings you conduct will be effective and well received.
- *Keep the meeting rules clear and simple.* Every meeting needs to have simple, clearly spoken rules that guide the way members behave. *As the facilitator, it is your job to make sure that everyone adheres to the rules of the meeting.* Rules that are not enforced are meaningless, and when this happens, it sends the message to campers that rules don't really matter.

Key point #44: Everyone has a place.

One critical aspect of every meeting is that everyone has a place. This practice is a subtle, but powerful, way of saying that everyone is an equal member of the cabin or group. Some kids come to a meeting and sit on another camper's lap. Others try to participate in the meeting from their bed or some other corner of the cabin or from outside the circle. *It is important that you as the counselor and facilitator of the meeting gently, but firmly, invite each and every camper to sit in their own space during the meeting.* The language I use when I am addressing someone who wants to remain outside the circle is, "No, it's okay, everyone has a place in our group. You can come down and join us." For campers who want to sit on a friend's lap I say something like, "I want everyone to have their own spot in the meeting. You can sit together after we're finished. This won't take too long." In other words, you are gently assuring each camper that they have as legitimate a place in the group as any other camper, *even when they are telling you they don't care or would rather sit outside the circle.* To allow a camper to sit apart from the group is to confirm non-verbally that they are not full-fledged members of that group. That message is not something you want to project, if you want all your campers to feel welcome and included.

For very short meetings—ones that last less than two minutes, I am less strict about campers sitting on each other's laps, but I still want everyone down off their beds and in the circle.

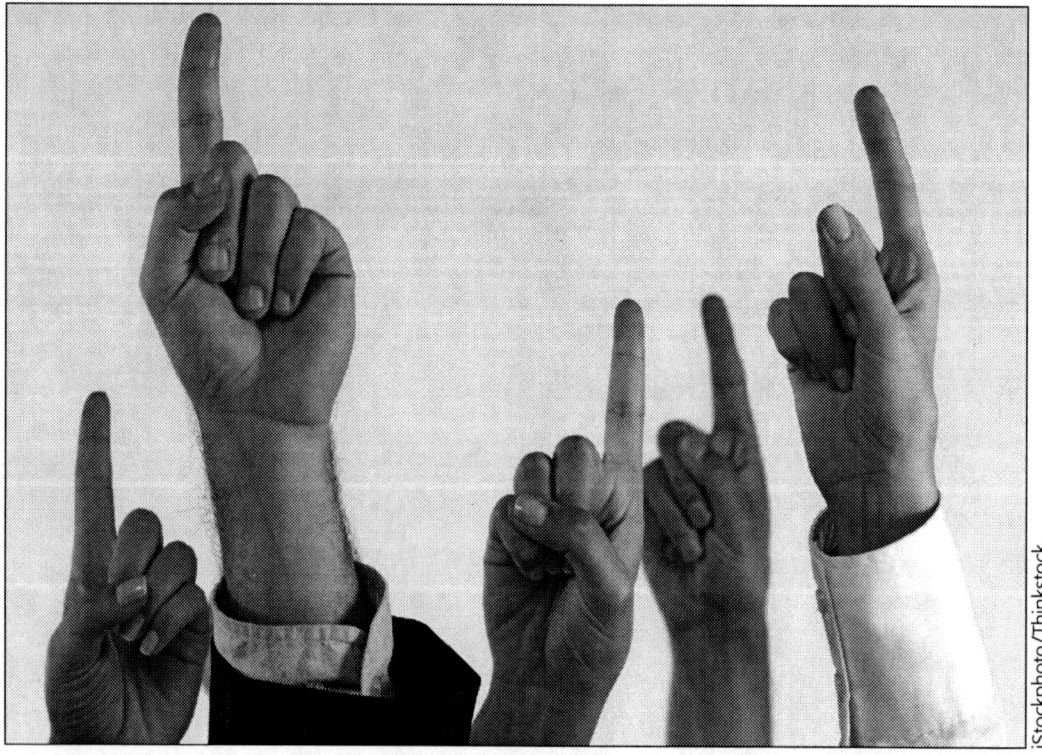

iStockphoto/Thinkstock

Key point #45: Counselors sit *across* from one another.

The best place for co-counselors to sit in group meetings is across from one another. If there are more than two of you, position yourselves evenly around the circle. Doing so means that you and your counselor colleagues will be able to see one another at all times during the meeting. It means that if you are missing what a camper is doing because they are sitting right next to you, the counselor across the way will see it even if you don't. It also means you will be able to catch the eye of your co-counselor(s) if you need to make a change in the agenda or make some other adjustment or address a certain issue. It also increases the likelihood that the two or three of you will talk to one another during the meeting—almost like thinking out loud. This practice is especially powerful, since it demonstrates to the campers that you as counselors are on the same page and work together effectively—an important message to give young people.

iStockphoto/Thinkstock

Key point #46: Essential meeting rules—the "envelope of safety"

Every meeting should abide by certain rules, including the following:
- Only one person speaks at a time. Everyone else listens.
- Campers wait to be called on by a counselor.
- Everyone speaks for him or herself.
- Everyone respects everyone else. You can disagree with what someone else says, as long as you do it respectfully. In other words, there are no "putdowns" in meetings.

There may be times when you may want to add another rule or two. For example, you may be having a meeting where it is important to agree that, "what gets said here, stays here." Or you may want to have everyone speak from the first person, using so-called "I-statements."

Whatever the rules are, it is best to have them written down and posted in a place where they can easily be repeated before each meeting and referred to during the meeting. As a facilitator of meetings, you are creating a set of expectations around the meetings that campers will be safe, orderly, and respectful. When everyone realizes and can count on safety and consistency, you will have successfully created what I call an "envelope of safety" in your group—a safe place where things can get talked about.

Key point #47: Using chips or tokens to take turns

Some campers are more articulate or more comfortable in meetings than others, and some campers are quieter or less self-confident in meetings. The danger in any meeting is that the more assertive children may make it more difficult for those campers who are less self-assured to speak up. A creative and practical way to solve this dilemma is to give each camper a small pinecone, a chip, or any token, which they place in the center of the meeting space when they wish to take a turn to talk. The rule is that you can only talk a second time (use your second chip or token) once everyone else has had a turn, as marked by the tokens.

The only way this rule can be effective is if you couple it with the two-minute rule: everyone gets two minutes to speak, before someone else gets a turn (you can adjust the time limit to fit the particular needs of your group). This practice helps keep the meeting from being dominated by one or two campers. On the other hand, as the counselor and facilitator, if you feel that a camper is in the middle of saying something that is particularly helpful or important for the group as a whole to hear, then you have the prerogative of extending that camper's time.

Make sure that each camper knows clearly what the time limit is for each turn. Knowing they have a time limit will help campers stop and think about what they want to say during their turn, rather than impulsively launching into their comments without thinking them through. This mindset may take a little practice because most kids are not used to meetings this systematic and precise.

iStockphoto/Thinkstock

Key point #48: The "talking stick"

Another effective and popular way of managing the conversation in meetings is to have a "talking stick" or similar item that you as the meeting facilitator control. Once the floor is open for general discussion, the counselor holding the talking stick passes it to the camper whose turn it is to speak. That camper puts their token into the center of the circle, takes the talking stick, and then shares. Once the camper is finished, they hand the object back to the *other* counselor (so that all the counselors are equally involved in the process). That counselor then chooses the next camper whose turn it is to share, and the process repeats.

The object can be anything that is easy to handle. I have seen counselors use a large conch or seashell, a large pinecone, a carved stick, a water bottle with the camp logo on it, or just a relatively stiff piece of paper with the cabin name on it.

One variation on the practice of counselors taking turns passing the talking stick back and forth is to have one counselor control the object for one entire meeting, then have another counselor control it for the next meeting, and so forth. Having the same counselor control the talking stick for the entire meeting may be less confusing to campers than passing it back and forth between different counselors. It is important that counselors switch off from meeting to meeting, however, in order to make it clear to the campers that each counselor has equal status as a leader in the group.

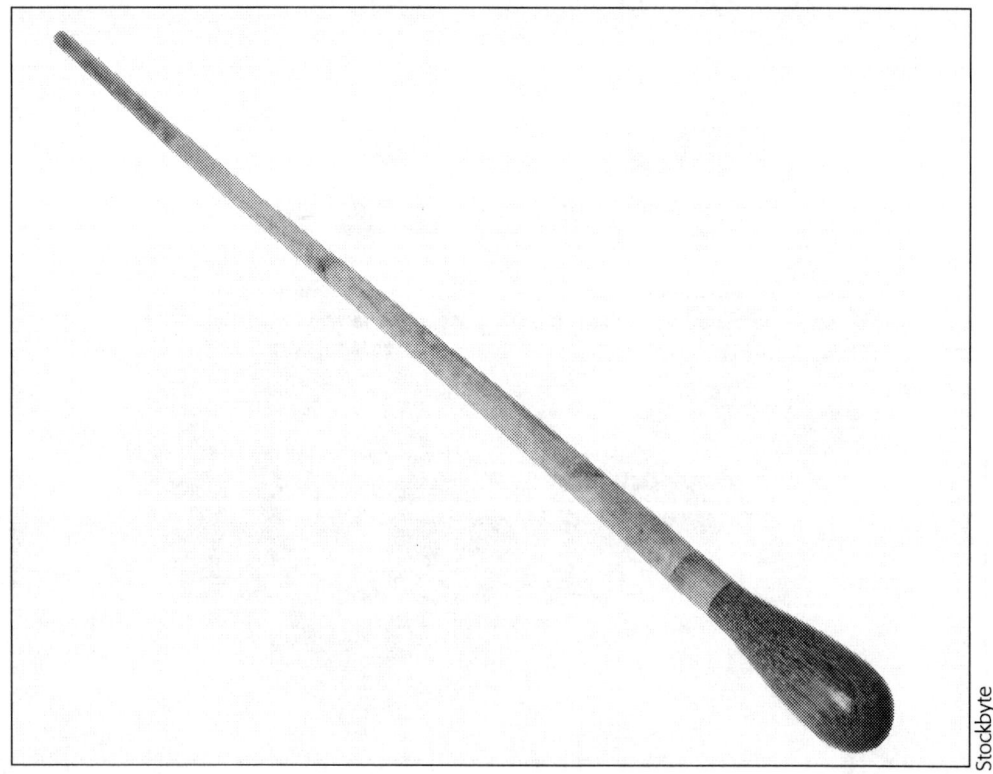

Stockbyte

Key point #49: Cabin or group agreements

Cabin or group agreements are an especially useful method of working with campers in groups. The underlying idea is to sit down with campers early in the session, after they have had a chance to get to know you as their counselor and have been at camp for part of a day. The purpose of the meeting is to come up with a set of agreements, generated by the campers, which they will live by during the rest of their time at camp. This step-by-step process, which counselors should practice during orientation by coming up with a version for staff, encompasses the following:

- Have the campers sit in a circle, each member with their own place.
- Counselors sit across from one another.
- Counselors announce the purpose of the meeting, which is to draw up a "cabin agreement." Counselors accomplish this by saying the following: "Guys, we are going to be living, working, and playing together for the next two weeks, so we need some agreements about how we are going to get along with one another, share space, and so on."
- Counselors use a large piece of newsprint or butcher block paper to write the following words at the top: "Everyone agrees…"
- Counselors then give an example of what an agreement might be and how it might be worded: "Ask before you borrow another person's stuff." Explain to the campers that agreements should be stated in simple, *positive* terms.
- Counselors quickly review the ground rules for cabin/group meetings (see point #46); they should then open up the discussion, asking the campers for their suggestions.
- Brainstorm a list of suggestions from the campers. The list is then edited by the counselors and pared down to just a few final agreements. A good number of agreements is from four to six, no more than seven. It is important that counselors make sure that two particular agreements are included in the final document: treat one another with respect and help each other out.
- The final list of agreements is posted in the cabin/group space with the group's name at the top.
- Give the agreement a name. Something like, "The Cabin 8 Pact."
- Every so often, counselors should sit down with campers to see what kind of a job they think they've been doing with regard to keeping the agreements. New stipulations can be added to the agreements, as needed. The objective is to revisit the agreement from time to time as a way of making it a living document, as well as serve as an ongoing reference point for guiding the way campers interact with one another during the summer.

Key point #50: The list of "firsts"

A cool thing to do with a group or cabin is to create what I call a "list of firsts." Any time a camper does something at camp they've never done before, like go waterskiing or down the zip line, or get on a horse or try out for a play, it gets written down on the list of firsts. This practice is a fun way to mark the activities of your campers and give them a chance to talk about the experiences they are having at camp.

The best way to mark new accomplishments on the list is to take a few minutes to meet briefly with the entire cabin or group, preferably at the end of the day, and have each camper share what it is they have done that day that is something they've never done before at camp. After they describe the activity, it gets written down on the list. Having a brief meeting, where campers share publicly with the rest of the group what they have done during the day, helps build unity and cohesion in the group. Otherwise the campers don't get the benefit of sharing with everyone in their group the new things that they have been doing. By doing it in the evening or at the end of the day at day camp, you help your campers get into a more reflective mood, one in which they can think about all the great things they have been experiencing at camp. It can even help campers identify things that they want to make sure they do before camp ends.

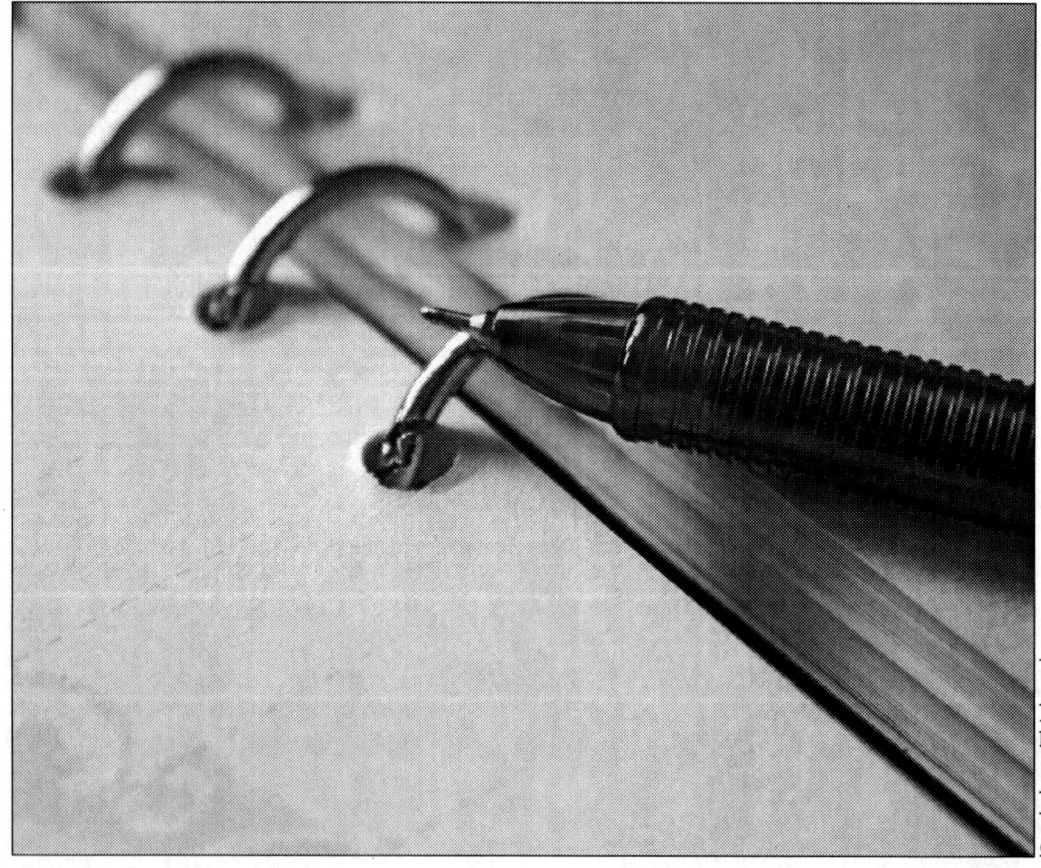

Key point #51: The job wheel

The job wheel is another device for working with campers in a group. All of the jobs that need to be done around the group meeting space or in the cabin, such as sweeping the floor, dusting, picking up trash around the outside of the cabin, emptying the trash containers or cleaning the sinks and toilets, can be written on the "wheel."

It is best to make the job wheel out of heavy stock paper, such as oak-tag. The jobs are written around the outside edge or circumference of the wheel. Another smaller wheel is then made with each camper's name written on it. The smaller wheel is attached to the larger wheel so that you can spin the inner wheel and match up each camper on the inside of the circle with a job on the outside of the circle.

This suggested strategy requires that there be as many jobs as there are campers. The way counselors handle this practice in larger cabins is they have two people sweep each day and two people picking up trash outside the cabin each day. You can even have one job space that says, "day off!" The underlying goal of the job wheel is to create a fair and dependable way to assign extra cleanup jobs to campers. While it is most effective when used with campers ages 6 to 12, even older campers may elect to have one.

The jobs assigned by the job wheel are in addition to the other "jobs" each camper has every day, like making their bed, putting their dirty laundry in their laundry bag, sweeping under their own bed, and making sure their cubby is neat.

Jupiterimages

Key point #52: The cleanup checklist

The cleanup checklist is a way to have campers take more initiative and ownership for the cleanup chores they are expected to do at camp every day. The underlying idea is simple: a chart is made with the names of every camper along the left side of the paper. You might consider including counselors on the list, so you can participate as well. Along the top of the page, you have the days of the week. Within each day you have the three or four things that every camper is expected to do for that day, like make their bed, sweep under their bed, put their dirty laundry away, and straighten their cubby. The sheet includes a column under each chore, day-by-day, so that each camper can find their own name, go across to the day of the week, and within that wider column, find the smaller column that corresponds to the job they just completed. Keep a pen or marker hanging on a string next to the chart, so that as each camper finishes a particular job for that day, they can walk over to the checklist and check that job off next to their name.

The cleanup checklist allows campers greater independence, while at the same time giving you, as the counselor, a quick moment-by-moment glance that indicates which campers are finished and which ones still have chores to complete for that day. The only time a camper should go on to the special job assigned to them for that day by the job wheel is when they have checked off all their other personal, daily chores on the checklist.

The job wheel works especially well with younger campers at resident camp, such as those ages 7 to 11. I use the checklist with the youngest campers as a way of praising their efforts: "Oh, look! Sally just checked off making her bed. Great going, Sally." This kind of praise works best with campers 7 to 9 or 10. Truth be known, praising teens in this way would undoubtedly cause a minor rebellion.

Key point #53: Beat the clock—make it a race against time.

Counselors are always looking for ways to make cleanup more enjoyable. One way to accomplish this goal is to occasionally play "beat the clock." It can be played one of two ways. The first is to have campers make a "bet" on how quickly they can all get their personal, daily chores done, and then start the clock to see if they can finish in the time they said they could.

A second way to play is to time the group during cleanup and then announce how much time they took when they are finished. The next day, the object of the game would be to beat their previous time. As the days pass by, the group can try to go for a "personal best group time," working to beat whatever their best time has been thus far.

Beat the clock works best with campers who are 8 to 11 years old. If campers are too young, they get frustrated when things take too long. If they are too old, they will view the game as childish and immature.

BananaStock

Key point #54:
The mayonnaise jar—public appreciation and gratitude

This group activity is a method for campers and counselors to publicly appreciate the good deeds of others. Publicly acknowledging or thanking others for what they have done for us or someone else is a great way to teach children gratitude. The "mayonnaise jar" does just that.

Children assemble in a comfortable meeting place, for example, on a porch or in a gazebo, where everyone fits comfortably and feels included. A leader asks for volunteers to stand up when called upon to publicly thank someone for something thoughtful or helpful that the person has done for them in the last day. The first time this exercise is undertaken, the leader may want to demonstrate how it works by going first. The leader would publicly acknowledge something helpful another counselor or a camper had done for them that day. In this instance, the following dialogue might be used: "I want to thank Sally for helping me find my clipboard this morning. Thanks, Sally, you were a great help. Please join me in thanking Sally."

Once the process has been explained and demonstrated by a few counselors, it is important to get the campers involved. Children catch on quickly. Remind them to say the child's name, to keep the exchange positive, and to say exactly what the child did to help them. Some campers will thank other kids for cheering them up when they were feeling sad, while others will thank kids for helping them with a chore or waiting up for them or inviting them to sit next to them. There may even be a time when a camper acknowledges a counselor. While counselors can always get the process started by going first, but it is always better to have campers do most of the sharing.

When someone is acknowledged, the group applauds that person. Although a person could stand up when recognized, through my many sessions in this activity, I have concluded that it goes more quickly and individual honorees are less likely to be embarrassed if they remain seated while the group applauds them.

The person who is recognized gets their name written on a piece of paper that is then put into a large clean jar. (Over the years, I have used a foodservice size mayonnaise jar for this purpose, thus the name of the exercise.) Every three to five days, names are drawn from the jar for small prizes. Prizes might be an extra canteen, a camp bracelet, a smiley face or fuzzy, or a camp pencil.

The mayonnaise jar emphasizes the kindness people show one another at camp. It provides a forum for children to express their thanks and practice gratitude. It is best done every day at the same time so that campers come to see it as a regular part of camp. Being publicly recognized by one's peers is probably enough of a reward in itself, without adding the small prizes. The drawing is only a ritual that serves to reinforce the value placed on cooperation, helpfulness, and the power of positive recognition. The exercise is a great way to create a more positive camp culture, based on gratitude.

Key point #55: Flashlight time

At the end of the day, once lights are out at resident camp, "flashlight time" is a bonus or reward for campers for their cooperating during bedtime. If your campers can be ready for bed by the time "lights out" occurs, then they get flashlight time. Being ready means doing everything they need to do to be ready for bed, like brushing teeth, changing their clothes, and tidying up. If that occurs, then a certain amount of time is allotted for using their flashlight to quietly read or draw or do whatever they want, as long as they are quiet and remain in their beds.

With younger children, ages 7 to 10, it can be used as a quid pro quo: you get ready for bed and the reward is yours. It has great appeal because most kids are keen to stay up as late as they can.

For older campers, I suggest staying out of this arrangement, since it will seem to them like you are treating them like young children. For them, flashlight time should be a set time that begins as soon as lights are out. Lights go out when everyone is ready and in bed. If campers use that time to prolong getting ready for bed, then they are simply cutting into their flashlight time. Your job is simply to keep time and hold them to the agreement. How much flashlight time they get is based on how well they manage their time.

One potential problem with flashlight time is when one or two campers are consistently late, while the others are ready. My suggestion is not to punish the entire group for the sins of the few—a common mistake made by some counselors. I would treat those one or two campers separately, attending to them as needed, with the consequence being that they forfeit whatever portion of their own flashlight time they use getting ready for bed. While you are dealing with them, everyone else will be enjoying the flashlight time they earned for themselves by being ready and cooperative.

Like bedtimes in general, the length of flashlight time should be adjusted according to the age of your campers. Older campers naturally go to bed later, because their brain chemistry—notably the melatonin cycle—dictates their sleep cycle; they get tired later than younger children or most adults. (That same brain chemistry will also dictate a teen's desire to get up later, too.) It makes sense to have flashlight time for younger campers to be something on the order of 10 minutes. For teens, 30 minutes is not out of the question, depending on what time you have lights out and what time they need to be up in the morning.

Key point #56: Nighttime check-in—flashlight etiquette

Another more interactive way to use the time just after lights out is to hold what I call a nighttime check-in. The way that this practice works is that every camper gets their flashlight and keeps it turned off until it is their turn. The counselor goes around to each camper and asks them to hold their flashlight under their chin and turn it on under their face. With the rest of the cabin dark, that camper now has everyone's attention. The "spotlight" is literally on them. The counselor asks that camper to share a moment from the day that was either the most fun or exciting for them or a time when they felt close to a friend or the rest of the group. If you have time, you might want to ask a follow-up question, for example, what one thing are they most looking forward to tomorrow?

One challenge with flashlight time or nighttime check-in is that campers sometimes have a tendency to turn their flashlights on when it is not their turn or shine their flashlight directly into the eyes of another camper. As a result, it is important that you explain beforehand that, while a flashlight is a camper's personal property, being able to use it is a privilege. Campers who misuse their flashlights have them taken away until they can agree to use them correctly.

The first time a camper misuses a flashlight, I suggest that you take it away until the end of that evening. If they have not already had their turn, they can get their flashlight back and go last. For a first-time offender, it is better to have them rejoin the group and be part of the activity, in order to lessen their embarrassment and allow them to make amends as soon as possible. Otherwise, you risk alienating them and causing a bigger problem than the one you are trying to solve. Handling it this way also shows the rest of your campers that you are a reasonable person.

If this misuse is a repeat offense, the camper should lose the flashlight until the next morning. If the pattern continues, it is time for a "walk and talk" (see Key point #31) or the respect conversation (see Key point #34).

Jupiterimages

Key point #57: Countdowns

An extremely valuable practice with groups is what I call a "countdown." Children have a tendency to become absorbed in the moment. In other words, most of them get so caught up in what they are doing that they lose track of time. This ability to become absorbed in an activity is called "flow experience." I call it play with abandon. You can see flow experience when kids are highly engaged in a board game, a sporting competition, or wrapped up in some other engrossing activity, like spontaneous imaginative play. The fact that children achieve flow is one of the great things about camp. Getting them out of it is sometimes a challenge.

A countdown is when you start announcing the impending end of an activity period. "Okay, kids! We have five minutes before we clean up!"

Notice that the warning is timed to account for the clean-up time that might be required at the end of an activity, like putting supplies away or spending time on debriefing, and not simply on the ending time of the activity period. In my experience, countdowns are useful with campers of any age—even adults. With younger campers you may actually want to give a minute-by-minute countdown. "Okay, we now have only four minutes until we have to start cleaning up!"

The alternative to using countdowns is getting into deal-making with kids. "Oh, just one more minute! I just need to do one more thing!" For a child who is waiting their turn in a sporting event, or when there is a close game, or when a child is making something they really like, getting them to give it up is tough. Simply announcing that their time is up is too abrupt and jarring for most children. Countdowns help by getting kids ready to get ready.

In the National Football League, there is something called the "two-minute warning." During this period, the game officials blow their whistles, the game clock is stopped, and the teams change players on the field. It is like the officials are saying to both teams, "Guys, you have two minutes before the game ends. Get your act together!" Frankly, I say if it is good enough for the NFL, it is good enough for camp!

Key point #58: The well-placed "raid" or escapade

One of the most fun parts of camp is when counselors take campers on "raids." I use the word in quotes because most raids these days are, unbeknownst to campers, prearranged by the staff. Raids are not about destroying other cabins or stealing things. They are about being on a clandestine escapade, usually at night when campers think they may get into trouble if they get caught out of their cabins. A raid, in other words, is safe risk-taking.

Some camps prohibit the use of raids, because they are concerned that they might be teaching kids that breaking the rules is fun. Personally, I think kids have the ability to make distinctions between a special event and business as usual. As long as the raid does not involve the destruction of property or anyone getting hurt, they can be a great bonding exercise for a group of campers. The following true story about a raid I helped design will show you what I mean:

Several years ago, when I was visiting a camp in Maine, I heard about a group of 13-year-old boys in a cabin who were having a hard time getting along with one another. They were teasing and razzing each other, playing pranks and having what seemed like endless petty arguments with one another. It was clear they were not bonding as a group.

When I spoke with the directors about it, I suggested a well-planned escapade. The directors demurred, saying they did not believe in such things for the reasons I previously noted—namely, they did not want to risk having counselors teaching campers that breaking the rules by being out late at night was cool. In addition, they were concerned about the physical liability posed by having campers running about in the dark, especially in a state of excitement, where their judgment might not be so good.

I acknowledged these points, and then I asked them how serious they considered the situation with these 13-year-olds to be. They told me they had never seen a group so fragmented. They were concerned that the boys were having such a bad time that they might not ever want to come back to camp. I countered by saying that extraordinary circumstances warranted extraordinary measures. I then asked if I could dream up something that was safe, non-destructive, and highly manageable, would they consider it? They agreed.

The plan was for one of the counselors to gather a few supplies (e.g., some soft drinks, the making for s'mores and maybe some chips—food always being the way to the heart of a 13-year-old—and get them out to a campfire site just beyond the main camp. As far as the kids knew, the counselor was going on their night off. They had no idea what was being planned. As the evening activity drew to a close, the counselor who was "on" told the guys that he had something secret that he had been planning for the cabin, that it was critical that no one know about it, and that he would tell them once they got back to the cabin for bedtime. The campers' interest was clearly aroused. When they tried asking him what was up, he simply said he couldn't tell them until they were safely back at the cabin, because no one else could know. There is nothing that piques the interest of a teen better than telling them that you have something so secret to share with them, but that you can only do so under the most cautious of circumstances. They will practically beg you for the details!

Once they were back at the cabin, he told them to get their flashlights, turn off all of the cabin lights, and come sit in a circle. By now, the tension in the group was palpable. The counselor began. "As you guys know, they don't allow raids here at camp. You also know that if we get caught being out at night, we could get into serious trouble." (I suggested to the counselor that he purposely be vague about what that "serious trouble" might be.)

He continued, "But, I think the time has come for us to get out together and do something no other cabin has ever done before!" (Blazing a new trail has great appeal with teens, especially when it involves being up late at night.)

He explained that he couldn't tell them what he had planned, unless they all agreed to keep it a secret and to be as quiet and as covert as possible. Without their word, it just wasn't safe enough to proceed. It took two seconds for the boys to agree. This itself was a minor miracle, since they had never before agreed on anything since camp started.

The counselor then told the boys that the other counselor was, in fact, not on his night off but was waiting for them at a pre-determined location with soft drinks, chips, and a campfire. The location was far enough from camp that it probably wouldn't draw the attention of the directors or senior staff, but they had to be careful not to wake the other cabins up or draw attention to themselves in any way. The counselor then told the boys to dress in the darkest clothes they had and put on long pants and bug spray. He also produced a stick of black face paint, so he and each of the boys could blacken their faces—a gesture that only made the entire escapade seem that much more thrilling.

They were told that they couldn't bring flashlights and that before they could leave, they had to stuff their pillows under their covers, so that it looked like they were safely in their beds sleeping, just in case anyone came by to check. Once everyone was ready and the right time came, they all slipped quietly out of the cabin.

Once they wended their way through camp and got to the outer edge of the property, they could see the glow of a campfire. At one point the counselor said, "Let's run for it," at which point they all went into a gallop. They arrived at the campsite on the far end of the camp property to find the fire, the snacks, and a music box playing tunes. They couldn't believe it! Everyone was laughing about how they had pulled it off. The counselor who had been at the site waiting for them reminded the boys that the night was young and the possibility of getting caught still remained.

What the campers did not know was that the camp directors were entirely aware of the plan. They had even agreed with the counselors on what time the campers would leave the cabin. That's because the second part of the raid was about to begin. The directors waited enough time so that the campers had about 45 minutes at the campsite. They then headed out to the site themselves. Back at the site, the counselors had agreed that they would take turns serving as a lookout, "just in case" anyone came looking for them. And, of course, that is exactly what happened. The directors arrived and quietly let the "lookout" know they were there. The lookout then hurried back to the campfire and, in alarmed whispers, said that someone was coming and that they needed to get their things and get out. The counselors had anticipated this possible event with the campers and had made a plan about how to sneak back to the cabin in case they were discovered. The campers and the counselors quickly put the fire out with the bucket of water the lead counselor had provided when he made the fire in the fire ring. They grabbed their stuff and moved into the woods just off site. The director then stormed into the site demanding to know who was there. The kids scooted away in the dark, while the director made loud "discoveries" about someone having just been there because the fire was still hot.

The boys made it back to their cabin, with a mixture of relief, self-congratulations, and joy about having just pulled off the greatest escapade in camp history! They couldn't stop talking about it. At one point, the counselors called a huddle with the boys and, while congratulating them, made it clear that they had to keep news of their adventure to themselves. The next morning, as the boys were filing into the dining hall for breakfast, the camp directors, whose custom it was to greet the all the campers as they came in, called the counselors over to them. In a voice loud enough for the campers to hear, one of them asked whether they had heard anything unusual the night before. The directors let it be known that they knew someone had been out of their cabin but wasn't sure who it was. The counselor assured the directors he would let them know if he heard anything. You can imagine the excited whispers when he joined his cabin at their table a minute later! "OMG! We almost got caught! Do you think he knows! OMG!"

The escapade I have described in this instance was obviously complex and detailed. It involved some careful planning. Every detail related to safety was thought through, including having a bucket of water by the fire ring. It did create an enormously strong bond among the boys. The "raid" or adventure you plan can be much simpler. If you are going to do something like this, several simple guidelines can be helpful, including:

- The raid must be one in which the campers can be well managed and supervised. An activity that is planned with the purpose of helping the kids bond is obviously counterproductive if someone gets hurt.
- Any plan must be sanctioned by a camp director or a superior in charge. Any raid or adventure must have their approval. That approval must be obtained *before* you bring the possibility up with your campers.
- Every detail of the escapade must be carefully planned. Talk it through with your co-counselor or supervisor. The more carefully planned your event is, the safer it will be.
- The purpose of a raid or escapade is to strengthen the bond of your campers. No gain will occur if the bonding happens at the expense of other campers or camp members. Raids that cause damage to property or psyches are unhealthy and counterproductive.

Another example of a clever and safe raid is one that happened many years ago while I was assistant director of a boys sailing camp on Cape Cod. The director of a girls' sailing camp farther down the bay had called to ask about a raid her senior campers were planning on our camp. The girls had planned to sail up to our camp at night, moor their boats, and slip ashore undetected. They would then make their way to the dining hall, where they would completely set plates, glasses, and utensils on the tables for breakfast, papering the dining hall with toilet paper, and leaving a large sign just inside the entrance saying not only had they surprised us with this prank, but would surprise us later out on the bay by beating us in an upcoming regatta. "Caught you sleeping!" the sign said.

The director told us that her campers did not know she was calling, but she assured us that she had two of her most trustworthy counselors going with the girls and that they would take care not to do anything destructive or too risky.

So, with our blessing, which was given unbeknownst to either the girls or our boys, this good-natured prank went off with great impact. Although the girls didn't beat us in the regatta, they certainly made an impression with their "raid."

Doing something like this today would probably be hard to pull off, given the understandable concerns camp owners have about liability. On the other hand, you can see how a well thought-out, safe and well-planned escapade can be a great bonding experience for campers.

Jupiterimages

Key point #59: Rest-hour tournaments

Holding some kind of tournament during rest hour is a great undertaking for a group of campers. The tournament can actually have different games going at the same time, like Connect Four® and Stratego®, or checkers and jacks. The primary objective of the tournament is to provide some quiet time activity that still engages campers, but is low key and a break from the more physical action that is typically an aspect of other camp activities. Counselors create a tournament chart, and campers can elect to be a part of as many of the games as they want. With a wide range of possible games, for example, a board game, cards, jacks, or marbles, you can find something that will appeal to just about everyone in your group.

David De Lossy

Key point #60: "Bloody knuckles"

Children play some activities that involve someone being hit or hurt by the other kids. The card game "bloody knuckles" is a perfect example of a game that is not appropriate at camp. At the end of the game, when one of the players has won all of the cards and is holding the entire deck, they are supposed to "certify" their victory by smashing the deck on the other kid's knuckles. I was once seeing a boy in my psychotherapy practice who had learned the game at camp. He came back at the end of the summer and showed me how to play. When it came time to smash him on the knuckles (I had won the first round), I thought to myself, "How does it look for someone who is supposed to be a healer to smash a kid on his knuckles?"

There are a variety of "tough" games like this that boys play. For example, boys in high school play a game where one kids puts his knuckles down on a table while another whips a coin in his direction, aiming at the kid's knuckles.

My opinion is that these rough playground games, in which its a mark of winning to ultimately hurt your opponent, have no place in camp. While no doubt a variation of "bloody knuckles" exists that does not result in actual blood, a game like this has no place in the world of camp, where kids are being taught more cooperative and supportive ways of behaving with one another. These games should be left at home or on the playground.

iStockphoto/Thinkstock

Key point #61: Building momentum—gearing up for action

Building momentum is an extremely useful practice with groups of kids. It is used for making a transition from a quiet-time activity or a resting mode to a more energetic one. The most common situation where building momentum can be helpful is in getting kids up in the morning.

While some younger kids get up at the crack of dawn, most campers have trouble getting out of bed in the morning. Given that the activity level at camp is much higher than many of them are used to, many campers get tired after a few days at camp. Building momentum at wake up time might include the following steps:

- Have the counselors get up first and get dressed, which will enable them to give their full attention to the task of waking up and greeting their campers for the new day. Their activity will also begin to stir some of the campers.
- Put on some music. It should not be loud or jarring, but happy and upbeat. Assaulting your campers will only make them dig deeper into their sheets. The idea is to slowly increase the noise and activity level (e.g., build momentum), so that getting your campers up will become progressively easier.
- Get the kids going who are easier to get up and who offer less resistance. This step will not only add to the activity level in the cabin, it will also allow you to give your undivided attention to those campers who have a harder time complying.
- Rub the upper back of a camper who is having trouble waking up. Again, no rough treatment, just a simple rubbing of the upper back to stimulate blood flow and help wake the camper.

Part of building momentum is keeping things positive. Pulling the sheets off a camper or pouring water on them or threatening them are not examples of building momentum. Such steps are abusive and have no place in camp. If you have trouble getting a particular camper out of bed day after day, consult with your supervisor about other possible approaches.

Using the aforementioned principles, you can adapt the step-by-step process of building momentum to fit other situations, like getting kids up from rest hour to get ready for their afternoon activities. In this case, remember to use some of the other pointers that have already been reviewed, like countdowns (Key point #57) and pivoting (Key point #28).

Key point #62: Lowering momentum—coming down off "high energy"

Just as campers sometimes need to go from a quiet or resting state to a more active one, times will exist when they will be full of energy and enthusiasm and need to quiet down. An example of this situation would be coming off the field in the evening, having just played a spirited game of capture the flag, then heading into the cabin, and getting ready for bed. Good luck!

First of all, when kids are excited and stimulated from a game or activity in which they have just engaged, their adrenalin levels are high. Adrenalin is the body hormone that increases heart rate and blood flow, dilates blood vessels, and generally causes a state of high alertness in people. It is naturally produced by the adrenal glands during times of physical exertion or exhilarating activity. Once our adrenalin levels are up, it takes several minutes for them to drop back down, which is the underlying scientific reasoning behind the notion that it is folly to try to put kids to bed immediately after they have been running around or engaging in a highly active or exhilarating activity.

Lowering or reducing momentum is basically doing what it takes to allow adrenalin to recede in the body. Giving campers a chance to talk excitedly about the game they just played or recap the plays they made or the close calls in the game are all good examples of ways we can provide them with an opportunity to catch their breath. Getting them into the cabin and letting them get a drink of water, move around, find their stuff, change—anything minimally active so that it does not increase the adrenalin level—are all examples of lowering momentum. Once kids stop sweating and their heart rates drop, usually in about 10 to 15 minutes, you can make the transition to something quieter or more reflective, like sitting down to do the "list of firsts" (Key point #50), brushing their teeth, or settling down for bed.

If you do not give campers a chance to lower their momentum, you are simply setting them (and yourself) up for trouble. As science tells us, kids can't change moods on a dime. Giving them 10 minutes will make the next hour you spend with them much easier.

Key point #63: Sharing chart

It seems to me that in the past few years, that many campers have had difficulty sharing at camp. Whether it is the space around their bed, their counselor's time or attention, their things, or their friends, a lot of campers struggle with the close proximity that comes from living with a lot of other kids. While the exact reasons for this trend are not known, it is true that children today come from generally smaller families and often don't have to share things at home with a lot of brothers and sisters. Add to this the fact that children spend less time with one another engaged in spontaneous play and more time sitting in front of a screen of one sort or another, and it is no surprise that when they get to camp they have trouble sharing.

The sharing chart is designed to help campers develop a more cooperative attitude with regard to sharing. It is best used with campers, ages 8 to 12. Developing the chart is a six-step process:

- Step 1: Gather the campers in a circle. Establish ground rules for the meeting (see Key point #46), and explain that everyone seems to need help with sharing. Bring up examples of specific times when campers have had trouble sharing, whether it was letting other kids sit on their beds or use their things or sharing a game in the cabin.

- Step 2: Brainstorm a list with the campers of all the ways that they can share. Start by saying, "If you were all best friends, and I was to come by the cabin and watch you for a while, what kinds of things would I see you sharing?" Put a piece of newsprint up, where everyone can see it, and write down the things they come up with in response to this question. There will be things like sharing food, sharing equipment or belongings, sharing clothes, sharing jokes, sharing secrets or personal stories, sharing time, and sharing energy (like helping people out during cabin cleanup). Mention how, while these are all great examples of sharing, some of them, like sharing friends or your time, are somehow worth more than sharing "stuff."

- Step 3: Make a condensed list of the various ways campers can share with one another and weight each example. Things like sharing food or toys or equipment get one point, while sharing your time or your friends, your energy, or your personal space (such as letting someone sit on your bed) gets two or three points.

- Step 4: Make a chart and put every camper's name on it. Create spaces for every day for the next five or seven days, with two spaces for each day (10 to 14 spaces in all). The spaces are for recording scores for points that campers are about to learn how to earn.

- Step 5: Explain that twice a day, once at the beginning of rest hour and once in the evening, everyone will sit down in a meeting together. Campers will take turns reporting to the group anyone who has shared with them in some way during the preceding half day. A hypothetical example would be if Josh, one of the campers in the cabin, speaks up and says, "I want to thank Mark for sharing his time with me this morning during cleanup. He helped me clean my space." Josh not only thanks the kid who helped him, but he also gives a brief description of what it was Mark did to help him. Mark, the helper, then gets two points put next to his name on the chart. In this waym Mark has just earned two points for the group. It is important to explain clearly to campers that they earn points only when someone else in the cabin recognizes the sharing they did and that the points are earned for the group as a whole.

- Step 6: Set a target of a certain number of points that the group needs to earn in order for the entire group to "win" a special activity. That activity should be discussed beforehand so that each camper knows what it is they are working for. Examples of appropriate activities might include things like the following: a pool party with special snacks or pizza, a nighttime movie and popcorn, a campfire with hotdogs and/or marshmallows, a special hike with lunch on the trail, an extra period at the water park or other favorite activity, and a sleep out with other extras. The activity is a celebration more than a reward. It is something fun that the campers will all share. Only the campers who have earned points for the group can participate in the prize. (Counselors will need to do their fair share of encouraging and coaching campers to participate, especially if they see that a camper hasn't earned any points.) The activity can be enhanced by adopting a few other details, including:

  ✓ Everyone who has earned a point for the group gets to participate in the special activity. The target points (i.e., the number of points needed to earn the targeted activity) should be set by the counselors. The first target should be one point for each camper, multiplied by six times the number of campers in the group. For example, if there are eight campers, the first target should be 48 points. A group can reasonably be expected to hit that target in three days.

  ✓ Counselors must be ready to prompt campers during the day (e.g., "Hey, this would be a great time to earn a couple of sharing points for the group!"). Counselors will need to keep track of how things are going, so that if a camper has not earned any points for themselves after a day or two, the counselors can subtly prompt that camper to share.

  ✓ Negative behavior should be dealt with separately and not be mixed in with the sharing chart. An exception would be if the entire group of campers destroyed camp property or broke a major camp rule. In that case, the chart would need to be re-thought. One option would be to reset the count to zero points and have a fresh start.

  ✓ A camper who has shared noticeably more than other campers (and who therefore will have earned more points) might get a special privilege or some kind of special recognition. This factor, however, should be addressed after the target has been reached and not announced beforehand. Otherwise, things may devolve into a competition among campers in a way that would detract from the genuine sharing.

Key point #64: Closing circle

Closing circle is a group exercise or meeting designed to help people process, share, or debrief an experience they have had at camp. It can be used either to debrief a single event, like a trip or a hike, or for bringing closure to an entire camp session. It is a journal exercise that is great for groups who don't have much experience using journals, because the writing is minimal. It can be used once or repeated many times.

It is important to let participants know how you will be using closing circle. I usually tell the campers that their circle is private and will not be collected, but that everyone is expected to share at least one thing with the group. On the other hand, you just might want to encourage campers to share their actual physical "circle" with one another, something that is made out of heavy stock paper, just as many kids do with school yearbooks. Using it that way, they can write notes or messages on each other's circles and keep them as a memento of camp.

How It Works:

Distribute one circle (an actual cut-out or page with a circle drawn on it, divided into distinct sections or "wedges") to each group member. Explain what the group discussion will be about. For example, if you have just come off of a canoe trip with a group of campers, you would say, "I want to spend some time talking about the canoeing trip." If you are using it as an end-of-the-summer exercise, you would say, "This is a way for us to talk about and share our feelings about the whole summer."

Ask participants to label each wedge (refer to the accompanying list). Each wedge represents a category of a reflection, self-observation, feeling, or experience and acts as a "marker" for the experience the group is debriefing. Going back to the example of the canoe trip, you would make a paper circle for each camper who went on the trip. Each circle would be divided like a pie into wedges. In each wedge, you would write a category, chosen from the menu of suggested categories. You then sit down with the group, give each one a circle, and explain the process. The circle helps participants remember, reflect, and record their experiences and accompanying emotions. Among the suggested categories are the following:

• Something that surprised me about myself
• Something I accomplished
• A high point (of the trip/of the summer)
• A low point (of the trip/of the summer)
• A gift I received from the group
• A gift I gave an individual (or the group)
• A moment when I learned a new lesson about friendship
• Something I learned about myself
• A moment when our group felt the closest
• Something I didn't do that I wished I could have done

In the center of the circle, ask participants to draw a symbol that represents the overall experience for them. Once participants are writing, filling in the circle should take between 15 and 20 minutes.

When the group is finished, join in a circle, and share. The group focus seems better if you ask each person to share one thing from their own circle and continue around until everyone is finished with that category. Sharing more than one thing is optional. Generally, participants love to share and are happy to share everything they've written, but individuals should be allowed to "pass" if they do not wish to share from a particular category. It is best to set your ground rules or expectations around sharing, before you begin the exercise.

Depending upon how much time is allocated for sharing, with a group of 12, this activity should take about one hour. If the group is larger than 12, the activity will take longer. You may wish to let some of your older campers dwell a bit longer, as they are both more verbal and may have more reflecting to do, if this is one of their last years or sessions at camp, or if they just came back from a major trip or hike.

Variations:

Add your own categories. The purpose of this activity is to reflect on experiences and share them with group members. Be aware that different categories may affect the tone of the conversation. For example, if you want to create a more serious tone in the discussion, stay away from a category like "silliest moment." Another possible option would be, instead of using a circle, change the shape of the drawing to fit a theme. Use a tent shape if you've been on a camping experience; or use a boat or canoe shape if the group's been out on a trip involving the water. Call it "closing campfire!" Leave a wedge blank, and invite participants to fill in a category of their own choosing.

Hemera/Thinkstock

9

Mapping a Cabin or Group: Group Check-Ins, Getting Camper Feedback, Small Group Meetings*

*Portions of this chapter were previously published in the November/December 2009 issue of Camping Magazine in an article titled "Girls at Camp: Overcoming Relational Aggression." Those portions are reprinted here with permission from the magazine. This chapter is an elaboration of the some of the original content.

Mapping a cabin or group is a way to analyze the social dynamics within that group: who is friends with whom; where the conflicts in relationships are; what sub-groupings might exist; and who is feeling left out. Figuring out what the dynamics of a group is the first best step to figuring out how to intervene. Once you know who is aligned with whom, where the conflicts are, and who the true leaders are, you will have a better idea of where to focus your attention and just what you might need to do to obviate or prevent other battles.

I first thought of the idea while visiting a girls' resident camp in the Poconos in 2009. The camp had a cabin of girls who had been having a lot of conflict that summer, and by the time I got there, the counselors and the division leader were all at their wits' end. The relationships in this cabin seemed quite complex, which you will see once the map involving this group is reviewed later in this chapter. The counselors knew that fighting between two particular girls, who were close friends but always fought with one another, was causing a lot of stress in the group. Their fights, however, could not account for all of the strife that seemed to be present in the group. I decided I wanted to take my time to sort out the complex relationships, which is how I came upon the idea to "map" the cabin.

On the Case: Cabin Check-In

The first thing I do when I am trying to figure out the relationships in a group is to have what I call a "cabin check-in." This step offers a view of camp as seen through the eyes of the campers. I do the check-in without counselors present. I usually ask a division leader, unit director, or head counselor to accompany the girls so they won't be too uncomfortable meeting with someone who is a stranger to them. Once the girls are comfortable with me, I have the other adult leave.

I begin by introducing myself. "Hi! My name's Bob, and I am a friend of," and I mention the names of the camp directors. "I come to camp before the campers get here to train the staff and help them understand kids better and be the best counselors they can possibly be. Then, I come back to see how things are going. I do that by sitting down to talk with several different cabins (or groups at day camp) and see what's up."

When you do a cabin check-in, it is important to tell the campers right at the beginning of the meeting that they are not in trouble. "I'm just meeting with your cabin or group to get your ideas about how camp is going and how we can make it better." If the particular group you are meeting with has been experiencing a lot of conflict and has been having a lot of meetings as a result of those conflicts, they probably won't believe you. They will be convinced that you are really meeting with them because they are "the bad cabin," as one camper once said to me. No matter. Follow the group check-in as I describe it, and you will eventually disarm the campers and gain their trust.

Once I have introduced myself and explained the purpose of the meeting, I ask each camper to tell me her name, where she is from, and how long she's been coming to the camp. Sometimes, if the camper is new, I ask how she found out about camp. When the whole group is more comfortable, I ask them to tell me two or three things they like most about camp. "It can be anything," I say. Some kids say their favorite thing is being with their friends; some mention a particular activity or two; others talk about a favorite counselor. It only takes about 30 seconds for each child to tell me her favorite things, and by listening intently and making good eye contact, each camper begins to trust me more and more. Talking about what the girls like also helps, since it creates a positive tone in the discussion. Because I am giving them my undivided attention and hanging on every word they say, the girls begin to open up.

After everyone has had a chance to tell me their favorite things about camp, I repeat the same process by asking them to tell me one or two things they think would make their summer even better this year. Because I am asking them to be the experts about camp and again listening to every word they say, the trust I am building with them continues to gain momentum.

When everyone has shared their ideas with me, I tell them I am going to ask them a question on which I want them to vote. I first explain how they will vote. "Everyone holds up a closed fist and looks at me," I explain. Once I ask the question, the campers are to hold up either no fingers ("…that's keeping your fist closed and counts as a zero," I explain); or from one to five fingers, "Five being the best," I clarify. I demonstrate the voting method by using my own hand and hold up five fingers. "Remember," I say, "Five is the best," then, I fold my five fingers into a fist, "And this is a zero!" I tell them I want everyone to look at me while they are voting, because sometimes people look around to see how their friends are voting and then change their vote to be more like their friend's.

Once everyone has a grasp on the voting method, I ask the first question. "Tell me, using the scale of zero to five," I say, "how well you think everyone is getting along in the cabin. Okay, one, two, three, vote!"

You've got to be quick when you do this exercise, because the campers can't help but look around to see how their friends are voting and modify their responses to ally more closely with the way their friend is voting. Even this is revealing, since some girls all look to one or two girls, who are the individuals everyone looks to for approval. If, in the voting, I get a lot of twos and threes, I open it up. The group meeting ground rules (point #46) come in handy in this situation. "One person speaks at a time. Everyone else listens with respect. Speak for yourself. Wait until I call on you. No putdowns!"

I pursue the results by asking follow-up questions, such as, "So, tell me what's making you vote only a two or a three?" You must take care in this instance to tell the girls that this is not a time to criticize other members of their group. You just want to get some idea of where the problems are. I find that children today, both boys are girls, are very articulate. Most often, they will tell you where the trouble spots are in their group.

In the case of a cabin or group that is struggling to get along, I use the cabin check-in to gain entre to the group, build trust, and begin a conversation about their conflicts. Armed ahead of time with notes from the counselors, I already have an idea about which girls are fighting with which girls. I tell the girls—and this factor is important—that meeting with them as an entire group will not be effective, because there are different issues with different girls that need to be sorted out individually.

Mapping

The process of mapping a cabin or group starts with many small group meetings. While I have some idea about which sub-groups I should meet with, based on the notes from the counselors, I ask the girls to give me their opinion about whom I should meet with and in what combinations. Asking for their input gives them a sense of ownership in the process. They are, after all, the experts of their own group. I am just an outsider. For some of them, the fact that I am a man makes it even more interesting because, as one girl told me, "Guys don't always get girls!" They love the idea that I am going to try to "figure them out."

Creating the diagram or "map" offers a clear-eyed, non-emotional way of viewing the conflicts in the cabin. As you will see, it also serves as a guide for making helpful interventions. I tell the girls that I will meet with them after I have had a chance to do my evaluation. At that point, I present them with an actual diagram or "map" of their group, showing who is close to whom and who has conflicts with whom, which allows them to see whether I have gotten it right or not. The campers I have done this with have always been impressed by the fact I actually trying to figure them out. That interest—and intrigue—allows me to be pretty candid about what I find.

Figure 9-1 shows an actual "map" from the first cabin I mapped during the summer of 2009. It contains all of the elements used to map a group. Kelly and Bethany M. are

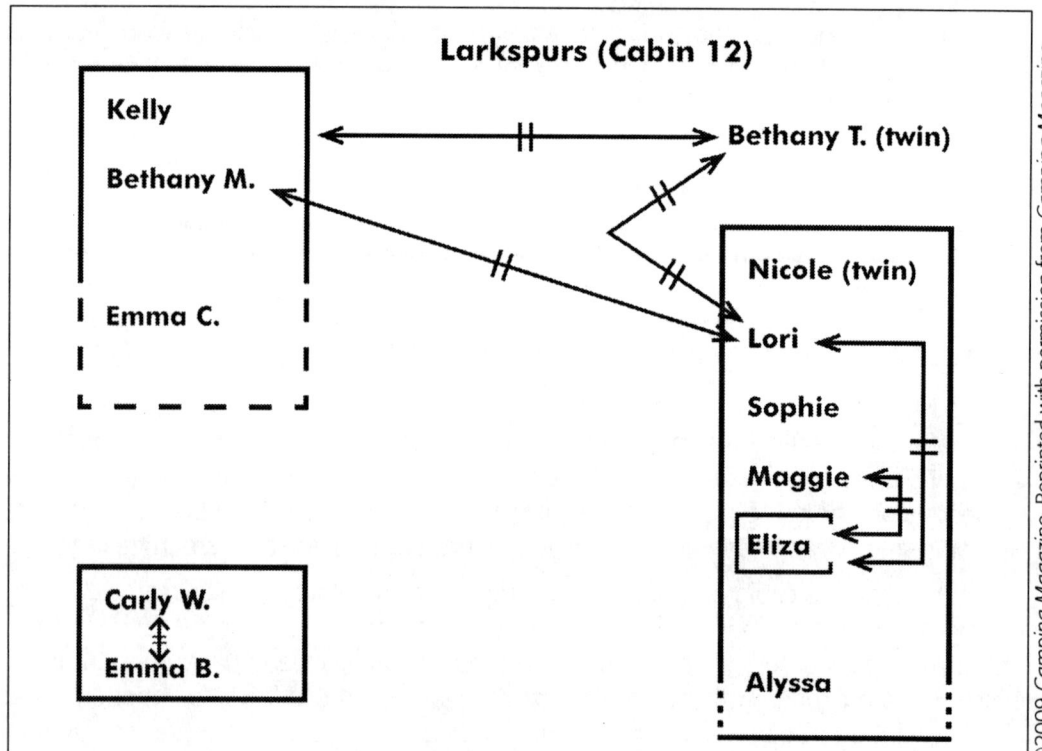

Figure 9-1.

from the same hometown and are very close in school. They are close at camp as well. Emma C. hangs out with them, which is why they are all in the same box. But, she isn't as close to them as they are to each other, which is indicated by the broken lines and the fact that her name is placed somewhat further away.

Bethany T. and Nicole are twins, also from the same town as Kelly and Bethany M. Nicole loves camp and is friends with everyone. Her twin, Bethany T., however, doesn't seem to fit in. Of the two, Nicole is more outgoing at camp, and Bethany T. is more reserved. Bethany T. is ambivalent about moving in on her sister's friends, even though her sister welcomes her. Bethany T. doesn't really get along with the two girls from her hometown. It would be logical to believe that it would be relatively easy for her to make friends with them, given that they go to the same school, but Bethany T. does not want to have anything to do with them. As a result, she is basically unconnected in this group.

Bethany T.'s lack of connection in the group turns out to be one of the destabilizing factors in the cabin; the more Bethany T. feels disconnected, the more hostile and disagreeable she is, which upsets the other girls. It also causes her sister, Nicole, to feel more responsible for her twin. The unhappier Bethany T. is, the more distracted and guilty Nicole feels. This finding had eluded the counselors and came to light only as a result of meeting in smaller groups, where the girls were able to describe and articulate the group's underlying dynamics to me.

Carly W. and Emma B. are both immature in different ways. Carly is developmentally behind the other girls. She is shorter, has not had her first menstrual period, and looks and acts much younger. She also has many fears, talks incessantly about her stuffed bear, and sings to herself—all traits that annoy the other girls. Emma B. is quiet and socially awkward, and she and Carly have a kind of love-hate relationship with one another. Emma feels stuck with Carly, who clings to her because the other girls leave her out. They fight constantly, and these fights also have a destabilizing influence on the group.

The counselors view Eliza as being very strong and often hurtful, in that she excludes girls from time to time and can make faces or spread rumors. It turns out that Eliza used to live in the same area as the other girls, but moved away two years ago. One reason she comes to this camp is to see her old friends. She is somewhat insecure, especially after having moved away, though she doesn't appear that way to the other girls. Nicole, Lori, Sophie, Maggie, Eliza, and Alyssa all hang out together, even though rifts often occur among them.

Once comfortable with me, Eliza was able to admit to me that when she is feeling uncertain about where she stands with the other girls, sometimes, without meaning to, she does things to try to keep them from connecting with one another. She fears the close relationship they may be developing, which makes her feel left out. When she is feeling this way, she might tell secrets or pull certain girls closer, while leaving others out—all in an attempt to control her standing within the group. Once she was able to admit this, she could tell some of her friends about how she has been feeling since she moved away. They were then moved to support her. This development had a very positive impact on the group and was a direct result of the mapping process.

Mapping as a Guide to Intervention

A cabin or group map serves as a guide to staff for making sensible interventions with the girls. For example, with this group, Carly and Emma B. need a vacation from one another from time to time, both for their sake and the sake of the overall mood in the cabin. We decided to find a younger camper from another group with whom Carly could have a play-date from time to time. It turned out that Emma had an older friend, also in another cabin. We set up a series of play dates between Emma and her friend. Undertaking this step not only gave Emma and Carly a break from one another, it also gave the group a break from the fighting in which the two of them so often engaged.

Bethany T. needs help making friends of her own, possibly with girls from another cabin. Eliza needs help talking to her friends when she feels insecure, rather than resorting to hurtful tactics. I actually helped her initiate this by meeting with her, two of her closest friends, and one of her counselors. Once Eliza could talk about her insecurity rather than telling secrets, or spreading rumors, the tension in the cabin was greatly reduced. The play-dates are the sorts of things that a head counselor, unit director, or division leader can easily arrange. Supporting Eliza by encouraging her to open up and be honest about her insecurity with her friends is something a sensitive counselor can easily initiate and manage.

When I showed the "map" to the girls, they were astounded. They couldn't figure out how a guy could "get them" so accurately. This type of relational mapping offers the girls the opportunity to acknowledge their group conflicts, because it allows them to understand them in simple terms. As a result, they can make efforts to change. Make no mistake, mapping a cabin or group is time intensive. It may take several meetings to get to the crux of the issue and find a solution. But as these examples show, it's well worth it. The girls take away something more emotionally rewarding from camp, along with the sense that somebody listened to them!

10

Contracting With Campers

Jupiterimages

Some children's behavior at camp is so challenging that it requires a more structured and formalized method of intervention. Children who consistently refuse to comply with the most basic aspects of camp, like listening to counselors, staying with their group, participating in activities, and treating others with respect, might benefit from being put on an agreement or contract. Children who do not abide by the basic tenets of camp do not usually respond in a positive manner when appealing to their sense of justice or their love of community. Having heart-to-heart talks with them is not enough "medicine" to manage their behavior.

Two different points in time actually occur when you might consider using a contract with a camper. The first is for a situation that involves a camper who was either sent home last summer and wants to return or who was able to make it to the end of the session last year, but only with an extraordinary effort on the part of the staff. I often joke and say that there are campers whose reputations precede them. Unfortunately, it is no joke if you are the counselor whose cabin or group to which this child is assigned. Nothing is worse for the morale of staff than the dread of knowing that you are the one who will have to work with a camper who has a reputation for being difficult to manage.

The second point in time to consider putting a camper on a contract is when a child is already at camp and is not responding to the interventions of anyone on the staff. Since camp is an elective endeavor, it is always possible to simply send the child home. However, if you think there is enough to work with and the conditions are right, putting a camper on an agreement just might work.

As noted, certain conditions must exist for the process of contracting with a camper to be successful. First, the child has got to want to be at camp. If the child is kicking and screaming, figuratively or literally, in order to be sent home, putting a contract in place will simply not work. If the child is not motivated to be at camp, they will not buy in to the terms of the agreement.

Second, the child must like some aspects of camp sufficiently enough to motivate the child to want to be at camp for an agreement to work. For example, the child might have friends at camp they want to be with, or they might have certain activities they love doing, or they might have a particular counselor they truly adore and want to be around. Again, if the child cannot identify *anything* at camp they want to do or anyone they like spending time with, then drawing up a contract will be a waste of time and energy.

The third thing you will need for a contract or agreement to work is a partnership with the camper's parents. Some parents are defensive about the way their child is behaving at camp. They try to blame it on the camp and often say something like, "It must be something you're doing there because we *never* have this kind of trouble with him!" If a child's parents are not on board, they will undermine anything you try to put in place.

Once parents realize, however, that you might just send their child home, they often become more cooperative and appreciative. I have also come across many parents who appreciate the fact that their child can be challenging and are grateful for the willingness of camp professionals to take the extra steps to help their child be more successful.

It must be made clear to the parents from the start, however, that creating an agreement or contract with their child is not a guarantee that their child will be successful or will be able to stay at camp. It is only an attempt to do whatever the camp can to help guide their child. It is their child's behavior that will determine the ultimate outcome of the agreement. Parents need to be assured that the contract will be kept as confidential as possible and shared only with their child, their child's cabin or group counselor, the counselor's supervisor, and the camp director. Parents will also want to know a few details about the contract before it is actually drawn up with the input of the child. You should share the following points with them:

- The child will be involved in the process of drawing up the agreement.
- The contract will require the child to comply with up to three specific targeted behaviors. (Prior to the contract being given to the child for a signature, you will let them know what the three behaviors are that you have in mind.)
- There will be positive consequences for the child if the child complies.
- There will be negative consequences if the child does not comply, which might culminate with the child being sent home.
- The parents will be given periodic progress reports about how their child is progressing.

The fourth condition for achieving success in the contractual process has to do with campers who are already in camp and whose behavior has been so offensive or upsetting that other campers are now feeling unsafe around them. If a camper has behaved in such a way that other campers or counselors don't feel safe, putting that camper on a contract may not be enough to reassure other members of the community that the child's behavior can be effectively managed. If this situation exists, then you have several issues to think about. First, you may be salvaging one camper only to lose several others in the process. Second, you may end up with a public relations crisis, especially if the parents of the other campers get the sense that this one camper threatens their children. In that case, it might just be too late to reclaim the situation.

The last set of possible circumstances that can impact whether contracting with a particular child will be successful concerns the seriousness of the child's behavior. If a camper has become so alienated or disregulated that they pose a threat to themselves or others, then you have a potential liability on your hands that may preclude keeping them at camp. A camper who cannot be managed can become a safety issue either by jeopardizing their own wellbeing or that of others. The checklist in Appendix B, titled "Signs of Distress at Camp" offers a useful reference for assessing whether the camp can reasonably and safely keep this child in camp. *If you have any concerns about emotional or physical safety, you should contact a licensed mental health worker who can consult with you about the camper.*

Contract Nuts and Bolts

- Most youngsters have a negative reaction to the idea of being on a "contract." Call it an agreement, which conveys a greater sense of partnership. After all, one key theme of camp is working with others. Entering an agreement is the start of working with others.

- A solid agreement is one that has both the parents' approval and the camper's input. Though you must have the parents blessing before you begin the process, you will actually need to engage the child without the parent in order for the agreement to work. After all, parents do not have to live with the agreement. You and the child do! To make it a workable document, you will need to have input from the camper, otherwise the child will not have a sense of ownership in the agreement and will not be motivated to comply with its terms.

- The first part of the agreement contains the specific behaviors the child agrees to while they are at camp. These "targeted behaviors" are the actual things the child agrees that they will do or say. They are stated in positive terms, are simple and clear, and are limited to a maximum of three. The following are just a few examples of target behaviors:

  ✓ Doing what your counselor asks you to do
  ✓ Participating in cleanup
  ✓ Staying with the group
  ✓ Participating in activities
  ✓ Getting help from a counselor when there is a conflict with another camper
  ✓ Being on time to activities
  ✓ Getting up on time in the morning
  ✓ Going to bed at night when "lights are out"
  ✓ Treating other campers with respect
  ✓ Keeping your hands to yourself

- The second part of the agreement outlines the positive consequences for compliance. For example, if the child demonstrates all of the behaviors that they have been asked to comply with, they can get some special one-on-one time with a favorite staff person. Another example of a positive consequence is to have extra time in a favorite activity, like horseback riding or waterskiing. Still another is to get first choice when signing up for electives. Yet another positive consequence, one that might be reserved for a very high level of success or compliance, is for the camper to earn a special activity for her cabin or group, like a movie at night with popcorn. Some camp professionals have worried that if one child is earning special privileges, other campers may become envious. My experience is that when campers know that a child is making an effort to be more civil, or less rude, or more fun to be around, they are relieved. In the face of that sense of relief, they don't feel so envious. Furthermore, if the child is so successful that they earn a special activity for the entire group, they become a hero, rather than the object of envy.

- The third part of the contract specifies the negative consequences for non-compliance. Negative consequences, like positive ones, should be progressive. In other words, the consequences are initially relatively mild and are increasingly more serious, in order to be commensurate with the child's lack of compliance. A first-level negative consequence might simply be to have a warning and a talk with the counselor and the counselor's supervisor. A second-level consequence might be to have to call the child's home. A third-level consequence might be to make an apology (to a camper or counselor), and then make some amends, such as doing an extra chore at cleanup or picking up trash around camp. A third-level consequence might be, for example, at day camp, to have to stay home for a day. At resident camp, it might be to have to spend half a day in a group of campers much younger or much older. A fourth-level negative consequence might be that the parents have to come pick the camper up. If the family lives within driving distance of camp, it is even possible that a fourth-level negative response would be for the child to go home for three days and think about whether they really want to come back, and if so, what exactly they are going to do to change their behavior.

A few special notes about contracting with a returning camper. If this process can be conducted in person (off-season), that makes it all the more effective. In some cases, when you cannot meet with the child face-to-face, creating the agreement may be done over the phone.

Start the process by explaining that you want the camper to be as successful at camp as they can be. Do not be shy about pointing out that she has had some difficulties in the past, but that you expect that they have experienced a year of growing up and that you want to believe in them and want to help them be successful and have fun at camp. Then, introduce the idea that having an agreement in place *before* they come to camp is the best way to insure that the process is successful. Also explain to them that you have spoken to their parents and that they are in full agreement with this process and arrangement.

I'd like to make one last point about camper compliance. If the child cannot comply, they are telling us through their behavior that they are not ready to be at camp. They can only remain at camp if they are willing to make a true effort at complying with the terms of the agreement. This point must also be made clear to parents at the beginning of the process. Even though you are working for success, if the child's behavior tells us that they are not ready for or do not want to be at camp, you must follow through and send them home.

- The final step in the process is to have everyone sign the agreement, including the camper. If the agreement is being drawn up before camp, then it is best done in the presence of the child's parents. If the agreement has been drawn up at camp, it should be signed by the camper, the counselors, the supervisor, and the camp director. It should be reiterated to the child at the time of the signing that everyone is cheering for them and their success. Everyone is willing to work with them if they are willing to put in a good faith effort. However, it must be made clear that the final outcome of the process rests with the camper. The child will let everyone know how much they want to stay at camp by how they behave.

APPENDIX A: Ready, Set, Go!
Five Areas of Readiness for Camp

Self-Care Habits

	Yes	No
Your child is able to choose and put on his/her own clothes.	❏	❏
Your child is able to brush their teeth without a lot of prompting.	❏	❏
Your child washes up or gets clean without a lot of prompting.	❏	❏
Your child has taken a shower on their own.	❏	❏
Your child generally sleeps through the night.	❏	❏
Your child does not usually have severe nightmares.	❏	❏
Your child rarely wets him or herself at night or during the day.	❏	❏
Your child agreeably wears clothing that fits the weather.	❏	❏
Your child can ask for help around self-care issues (dressing, eating, bathroom care, showering, etc.)	❏	❏

Family Relationships

	Yes	No
Is your child able to ask for help from you or another significant adult in his or her life when he or she has a problem at home or in school?	❏	❏
Does your child usually obey your requests and follow rules in your household?	❏	❏
Does your child have a positive, nurturing relationship with at least one grandparent?	❏	❏
Has your child successfully slept over at a relative's house?	❏	❏

Friendships/Social Relationships

	Yes	No
Does your child have a best friend?	❏	❏
Does your child make and get phone calls from kids his/her age?	❏	❏
Does your child get invited to play dates?	❏	❏
Does your child get invited to birthday parties/Bar and Bat Mitzvahs?	❏	❏
Has your child successfully slept over at a friend's house?	❏	❏
Has your child had any friends sleep over at your house?	❏	❏
Do other children want to come to your child's birthday parties?	❏	❏
Does your child play primarily with children the same age as him/herself?	❏	❏
Does your child share control of the play when he/she is with other children (the choices of games/the conversation/rules)?	❏	❏

School/Activities

	Yes	No
Does your child go to school with reasonable ease?	❏	❏
Does your child do reasonably well academically?	❏	❏
Does your child have friends in school?	❏	❏
Does your child follow school rules/comply with discipline?	❏	❏
Overall, is your child happy at school?	❏	❏
If your child is on an Individualized Education Plan (IEP), does he or she participate reasonably well with its provisions?	❏	❏

Overall Psychological Health

	Yes	No
Does your child recover from setbacks reasonably well?	❏	❏
Is your child able to express his or her feelings or concerns in words reasonably well?	❏	❏
When your child is upset does he or she eventually ask for and accept help?	❏	❏
Does your child eventually accept discipline reasonably well?	❏	❏
If your child has a problem has he or she been able to collaborate on problem-solving with a trusted adult in his or her life?	❏	❏
Overall, is your child reasonably happy?	❏	❏

Special note about activities at some camps:

If the camp your child is considering has special program features, like tripping, hiking, rock-climbing, horseback riding, endurance swimming, or other activities that might require being in good physical shape, make sure to discuss thoroughly with the camp's directors whether these activities are appropriate for your child.

APPENDIX B: Signs of Distress at Camp

The Diagnostic and Statistical Manual of Mental Disorders, fourth edition, published by the American Psychiatric Association, has a section titled, "Global Assessment of Functioning (GAF)." Known to mental health professionals as "Axis V," it is used to assess an individual's overall level of functioning on a scale from 0 to 100. GAF looks at things like primary support group, social environment, educational or occupational issues and so on. Using this scheme as a foundation and adding what are called signs of ego functioning, we have created this inventory. Each section has sample behaviors that correspond to the following levels:

1) Well-adjusted, low distress level—little or no concern

2) Moderate distress level requiring assistance and monitoring by adult—some concern

3) Significant distress level requiring frequent one-on-one monitoring and prompting—high level of concern; requires special arrangements

4) Severe signs of distress requiring major intervention and/or departure from camp

Five Areas of Observation

Self-Care Habits

- Camper is able to dress appropriately with minimal prompting.
- Camper keeps his or her things reasonably well organized.
- Camper is able to brush teeth, wash up and generally clean up with minimal prompting.
- Camper sleeps with little if any disturbance or difficulty.
- Camper is eating a reasonable selection of food with little prompting or supervision.
- Camper has momentary feelings of sadness with regard to homesickness.
- Camper has regular bowel movements and urination.
- Camper needs moderate amount of prompting to get properly dressed.
- Camper is sloppy, but well within the range expected at his or her age.
- Camper needs moderate amount of prompting to maintain self-care habits.
- Camper has occasional sleep disturbance—wakes up from a bad dream; summons the counselor; has an occasional bedwetting "accident."
- Camper is a picky eater; needs help choosing foods and finishing meals.
- Camper is clingy and has many moments of tearful, sad homesick feelings.
- Camper has evidenced some difficulty with bowel movements or day time urination (occasional day time "accident" or minimal soiling).
- Camper needs one-on-one supervision and help in order to get dressed.
- Camper is more disorganized than most anyone in the cabin or group.
- Camper needs one-on-one supervision in order to wash up, get clean, brush teeth, etc.

- Camper has extreme difficulty falling asleep or has nightmares and is not rested during the day.
- Camper is distraught with feelings of desperation and panic (homesick).
- Camper is severely limited in food choices, is eating far too few calories for their level of activity, or is overly obsessed with food and eating all the time.
- Camper is constipated and/or having multiple daytime wetting "accidents."
- Camper is unable to dress self at all.
- Camper is disorganized to the point of being disoriented.
- Camper is not able to perform self-care even with one-on-one supervision.
- Camper has night terrors, extreme state of anxiety at bedtime; his or her night time disturbances are disruptive to other campers.
- Camper is not eating; is eating and purging after meals; has lost significant weight, is gorging; has stomach aches, is throwing up, has frequent headaches or other somatic complaints.
- Camper is having daytime soiling or multiple daytime urination "accidents" and/or constant nighttime "accidents."

Relationships With Staff

- Camper interacts comfortably with most counselors and is well connected to one or two in particular.
- Camper interacts only with one or two counselors exclusively.
- Camper isolates —does not connect with any counselors.
- Camper is argumentative, uncooperative or disruptive with counselors.
- Camper is totally off in his or her own world—no eye contact; has conversations with self; does not acknowledge the presence of others.
- Camper is verbally aggressive toward counselors and rejects any help or intervention on his or her behalf.
- Camper feels singled out and persecuted by counselors.
- Camper has physically assaulted counselors. Counselors do not feel safe.

Friendships/Social Relationships

- Camper interacts with most other campers.
- Camper interacts only with one or two other campers exclusively.
- Camper isolates —is not engaging with any other campers. (Sits away from others; does not make eye contact with others; plays by him or herself).
- Camper is totally off in his or her own world—no eye contact; has conversations with self; does not acknowledge the presence of others.
- Camper is aggressive toward other campers—physically threatening or establishing actual physical "barriers" between him or herself and others.

- Camper is hitting or physically assaulting others. Campers do not feel safe in his or her presence.
- Camper is evoking such rage in others that he or she is at risk of verbal or physical retaliation.

Activities

- Camper readily goes to activities and participates most of the time.
- Camper needs prompting to go to activities and sometimes sits out or participates only part of the time.
- Camper isolates —shows little or no interest in activities and needs one-on-one accompaniment to get to activities.
- Camper is vehemently opposed to going to activities and often runs away or disappears.
- Camper is destructive of materials or equipment at activities.
- Camper is verbally aggressive toward activity counselors or campers.
- Camper's behavior poses a safety risk at activities.

Coping Mechanisms

Level One: Well adjusted; healthy coping mechanisms

- Camper is good-natured and deals with emotional conflict or stress by using humor and other high level defenses such as the following:
  - ✓ Anticipation: considers possible emotional reactions or consequences in advance of an event.
  - ✓ Affiliation: turns to others for support.
  - ✓ Altruism: lends a helping hand to others.
  - ✓ Self-assertion: expresses thoughts and feelings in a non-coercive way.
  - ✓ Self-observation: reflects on his or her own thoughts and feelings.

Level Two: Moderate stress; less than ideal coping mechanisms

- Camper is occasionally irritable, moody or difficult to approach or engage. May use slightly less adaptive defenses such as the following:
  - ✓ Acting out: uses actions rather than words to deal with conflict or stress (teasing, jeering, yelling are, in this case, considered, "actions").
  - ✓ Devaluation: attributes exaggerated negative qualities to self or others.
  - ✓ Idealization: attributes exaggerated positive qualities to self and others.
  - ✓ Displacement: transfers feelings or reactions onto objects (yelling at a door or other object; attributing feelings to a puppet or picture or image).
  - ✓ Intellectualization: excessive use of abstract thinking to minimize or avoid feelings.

Level Three: Significant stress; more severe defenses

- Camper is showing signs of significant distress and may be isolating or engaging in more severe acts of aggression. The defenses employed at this level of distress are more primitive, as follows:
  - ✓ Acting out: a more severe version of acting out which may include verbal and physical threats and acts, like abusive name calling, swearing, etc.
  - ✓ Denial: refusal to acknowledge a painful aspect of reality or experience apparent to others.
  - ✓ Dissociation: a breakdown in memory or awareness (heavy daydreaming).
  - ✓ Help-rejecting/complaining: complaining and making overt requests for help that hide hostility which is expressed by rejecting suggestions, etc.
  - ✓ Reaction formation: actually forming a reaction against an idea or feeling that is unacceptable to the person (saying you hate drugs and would never use them because you are secretly interested; saying something is disgusting when you are secretly intrigued or interested).

Level Four: Extreme stress; most primitive defenses

- Camper is not functioning in many areas as noted above. The most primitive defenses are evident, as follows:
  - ✓ Autistic fantasy: Excessive daydreaming and internal fantasy as a substitute for human relationships.
  - ✓ Paranoid thinking: having thoughts or perceptions that others are out to harm you.
  - ✓ Repression: expels disturbing wishes, thoughts or experiences from memory or awareness.

Camper behavior may deteriorate over time. A significant change in behavior or coping mechanisms is usually a sign of significant stress. This includes an sudden increase in what may be expressed as homesickness after having made a successful adjustment to camp. When a change in stress levels occurs in a camper or staff member, it may be evidence of the following:

- Stressful news from home (death, divorce, impending loss, disease).
- Delayed reaction to a stressful situation that developed or existed before camp began.
- A major stressful event at camp (significant teasing, bullying; sexual or physical threat, intimidation or abuse not readily apparent to staff).
- Decompensation: a deterioration in the mental status and health of the camper due to fragile ego or emerging mental illness.

APPENDIX C: A Lexicon of "Ditterizations"

During the many years that I have worked with camp professionals, I have introduced a number of terms that have become part of what it means to "be Ditter-ized." The following is a list of some of those terms:

- *The Other Duffle Bag:* A figurative reference to the tasks of emotional development—or "growing up stuff"—that all children carry with them to camp or school. I tell counselors that it is inevitable that campers will "unpack" that duffel bag at camp. In other words, children will invariably behave in ways that will give counselors many opportunities to help them be better at things like waiting their turn, asking for or accepting help, supporting others, tolerating strong feelings, regulating their feelings and impulses, taking responsibility, making amends, and so on.

- *Emotional Baggage*: Similar to the previous term, the other duffel bag, but more specific. Emotional baggage refers to the unresolved issues each of us has as a result of our ongoing life experiences. It may be that some people, i.e., campers or counselors, have unresolved issues with authority; or they may have a harder time trusting others; or they may characteristically set their expectations too high with the result being that they often end up feeling disappointed much of the time; or they may be too hard on themselves when they make a mistake. Just as it is with the other duffel bag, that emotional baggage has a good chance of showing up at camp in the form of that person's behavior. Camp can be a place that offers a relatively better opportunity for several of these issues to get resolved, primarily through the countless positive experiences that individuals can have in the camp environment.

- *Envelope of Safety:* The term refers to the physically and emotionally safe environment that counselors and other adults establish and maintain at camp by upholding clear limits and well-defined boundaries.

- *Occupational Hazards of Working with Children:* Collectively, the term applies to the set of risks that individuals take by putting themselves in the company of children, who are by nature noisy, messy, impulsive, imperfect, dependent, and curious. Although I often discuss this matter in a somewhat tongue-in-cheek way, the "hazards" of working with children are quite real and include the following:

  ✓ Over-identifying with a child. When we identify too strongly with the struggles or characteristics of a particular child, it can affect our ability to keep our perspective and work with them objectively.

  ✓ *Regressive pull* occurs when the regressive or immature behavior of children whose company we are keeping exerts a downward pull on our own maturity level. The way I explain it to counselors is that regressive pull is when we start to look and act just like the kids—impulsive, messy, noisy, and so on.

  ✓ Making parents wrong. Because we can see things from the child's point of view, it is easy, and often a mistake, to blame parents for the child's struggles or poor behavior, even though we have no clue about that parent's reality. The dangers can range from not being able to acknowledge a parent's point of view to being unable to create a trusting, working relationship with them.

- *Partnering with Parents* is a term that refers to creating a positive, understanding working relationship with parents in the overall task of helping to raise their children.
- *Overstimulated:* When we get a child or group of children too excited or engage them in an activity that is so exhilarating that it makes it too hard for them to self-regulate or control their feelings, the child is said to be over-stimulated.
- *Better Brakes:* When youngsters can't control their impulses, I talk about as "not being able to stop." It is like the child doesn't have very good "brakes," or impulse control.
- *Regressive Pull:* Mentioned as part of the "occupational hazards of working with children," the concept is so important that it deserves its own listing. Regressive pull is when we revert to more childish behavior ourselves, partly as the result of being in the company of children. Regressive pull is a universal phenomenon. It can happen to anyone under the right conditions and is, therefore, something of which all childcare workers should be aware.
- *Parallel Process:* When we treat counselors the way we want them to treat campers—welcoming, supportive, respectful, yet holding them accountable, it is called "parallel process." When we create the same conditions with staff that they will be experiencing with campers, it is called parallel process. The term originally comes from psychoanalysis, when a therapist unwittingly recreates a dynamic or relationship issue with a supervisor that exists between that therapist and their patient. The belief in psychoanalysis is that when the supervisor works through the issue with the therapist, they are providing the therapist with an experience that will serve as a guide for working through the same conflict or issue with the patient. At camp, I often point out to camp directors that if they expect counselors to set reasonable limits with the campers, they must set reasonable limits with their staff.
- *"Dear Occupant":* The term refers to a situation when a child directs an attitude or feeling at an adult that has nothing to do with that adult, but is actually an expression of feeling they have for a significant other adult in their life. An example is when the children who attended America's Camp, the one-week long program held for children whose parents perished in the September 11 attacks, developed an inexplicably immediate, strong positive feeling for the male staff. We realized that the feelings of love and yearning these children had for their lost fathers were being played out with the counseling staff at camp. The term comes from bulk snail mail that arrives at your home having been addressed to "occupant." These strong feelings can either be positive, as is the case with the America's Camp children, or negative.
- *Money in the Bank* refers to the effort a counselor or other adult makes to "invest" in a relationship with a camper or child. It includes taking an interest in the child, spending time with them, keeping promises, making apologies when necessary, setting good limits and so on. Having "money in the bank" with a child means you have made enough of an investment in your relationship with them that you have "currency" or influence with them.

- *Drop the Rope:* Probably the most famous of the Bob Ditter lines, "drop the rope" means avoiding the power struggles in which children often try to ensnare us. A more comprehensive description of the concept and how you go about "dropping the rope" is presented in key point #13 in Chapter 6.

About the Author

Bob Ditter is a well-respected clinical social worker who specializes in the evaluation and treatment of children, adolescents, and their families. He maintains a psychotherapy practice in Boston, Massachusetts, and consults nationally with agencies that work with young people. Some of his clients have included the Salvation Army, the Girls Scouts of America, the YMCA, the American Camp Association, Jewish community centers, Sea World, the Disney Channel, private and public schools, and others. He has appeared on NBC's Today Show, the ABC Evening News with Peter Jennings, and Good Morning America. He has been quoted in the *New York Times, Parent* magazine, *Ladies Home Journal, Money* magazine, and *USA Today. Sports Illustrated* called him "camping's most articulate spokesman" because of his work with children's summer camps since 1982. He has authored several books and has been featured on numerous well-received DVDs for camp professionals. He is best known in camp circles as the author of the popular column, "In the Trenches," which has appeared regularly in *Camping Magazine* since 1987. Bob received the Hedley S. Dimock award, camping's highest honor, for his contributions to the field in 1992.